A Tale of Two Schools

NEW PERSPECTIVES ON LANGUAGE AND EDUCATION
Series Editor: Professor Viv Edwards, *University of Reading, Reading, Great Britain*
Series Advisor: Professor Allan Luke, *Queensland University of Technology, Brisbane, Australia*

Two decades of research and development in language and literacy education have yielded a broad, multidisciplinary focus. Yet education systems face constant economic and technological change, with attendant issues of identity and power, community and culture. This series will feature critical and interpretive, disciplinary and multidisciplinary perspectives on teaching and learning, language and literacy in new times.

Full details of all the books in this series and of all our other publications can be found on http://www.multilingual-matters.com, or by writing to Multilingual Matters, St Nicholas House, 31-34 High Street, Bristol BS1 2AW, UK.

NEW PERSPECTIVES ON LANGUAGE AND EDUCATION
Series Editor: Professor Viv Edwards, *University of Reading, Reading, Great Britain*

A Tale of Two Schools
Developing Sustainable Early Foreign Language Programs

Richard Donato and G. Richard Tucker

MULTILINGUAL MATTERS
Bristol • Buffalo • Toronto

Library of Congress Cataloging in Publication Data
A catalog record for this book is available from the Library of Congress.
Donato, Richard.
A Tale of Two Schools: Developing Sustainable Early Foreign Language Programs/
Richard Donato and G. Richard Tucker.
New Perspectives on Language and Education
Includes bibliographical references and index.
1. Language and languages–Programmed instruction. 2. Language and languages–
Study and teaching. 3. Children–Language. 4. Language acquisition. I. Tucker,
G. Richard. II. Title.
P53.D66 2010
372.65–dc22 2010026209

British Library Cataloguing in Publication Data
A catalogue entry for this book is available from the British Library.

ISBN-13: 978-1-84769-310-5 (hbk)
ISBN-13: 978-1-84769-309-9 (pbk)

Multilingual Matters
UK: St Nicholas House, 31-34 High Street, Bristol BS1 2AW, UK.
USA: UTP, 2250 Military Road, Tonawanda, NY 14150, USA
Canada: UTP, 5201 Dufferin Street, North York, Ontario M3H 5T8, Canada.

Copyright © 2010 Richard Donato and G. Richard Tucker

All rights reserved. No part of this work may be reproduced in any form or by any means without permission in writing from the publisher.

The policy of Multilingual Matters/Channel View Publications is to use papers that are natural, renewable and recyclable products, made from wood grown in sustainable forests. In the manufacturing process of our books, and to further support our policy, preference is given to printers that have FSC and PEFC Chain of Custody certification. The FSC and/or PEFC logos will appear on those books where full certification has been granted to the printer concerned.

Typeset by Datapage International Ltd.

Contents

1. Introduction: A Tale of Two Schools 1
   Rationale for this Monograph 1
   Essential Questions 6
   Brief Review of US Experiences. 9
   Brief Review of International Experiences 12

2. Program Development and Implementation:
   A Contrastive Story. 20
   The Japanese Program: 1992–2005. 20
   The Spanish Program: 1995–Present 24
   How Did the Program Begin? 29

3. A Comprehensive Model of Program Evaluation 33
   The Culture of Assessment and Foreign Language
   Education Programs 34
   Profiles of Success: Our Emerging Assessment Plan 35
   The Challenges of Conducting EFLL Research 35
   Programmatic Issues: Transitions and Connections 42
   Principles of Assessment. 45
   Areas of Assessment 48
   Summary. 57

4. Documenting Student Language Achievement 59
   Students' Cumulative Oral Language Development:
   Year 1 of JFL 60
   Students' Cumulative Oral Language Development:
   Year 3 of JFL 62
   Documenting JFL Vocabulary Development in Year 3 66
   Students' Cumulative Oral Language Development:
   Year 6 of JFL 68
   Students' Spanish Literacy Development over Time 72
   Relationships Between Classroom Instruction and
   Oral and Written Language Development 86

Relationships Between Classroom Discourse and
Student Independent Performance 89
Summary. 94

5 Documenting Language Program Development: The Views
of Parents, Children and their Teachers. 96
What Do Parents Expect their Children to Learn? 96
What are Students' Impressions of their Language Study? 103
What do Students Believe they can do with their
Languages? 109
The Role and the Contribution of a Foreign Language
in the Life of a School: Contrasting Experiences 113
The Foreign Language Teacher as Agent of Change 118
Summary. 121

6 The Sustainability of Early Language Learning Programs 123
Internal Conditions that Create Challenges 123
External Conditions that Create Challenges. 129
Summary. 134

7 Emergent Themes of Successful Programs. 137
The *Vision* for the Program 137
Support for the Teachers 140
Concern for Participating Students 142
Positioning the Program within the Life of the School. 144
Summary. 147

8 Summary and Conclusions 149
Lessons We Have Learned 149
Implications for Other Districts. 156
Implications for Additional Research. 157
Sustainable Development: An Environmental Perspective. . . . 159
Concluding Remarks. 163

Appendix A Modified ACTFL Rubric for the Presentational
Mode of Communication of Intermediate
Level Learners. 166
References 171
Index 178

Chapter 1
Introduction: A Tale of Two Schools

Rationale for this Monograph

Similar to Charles Dickens' novel, *A Tale of Two Cities*, creating and sustaining foreign language education programs for all children in the elementary grades can be viewed as 'the best of times and the worst of times'. Despite intense efforts by national organizations, such as the National Network for Early Language Learning (NNELL) and the American Council on the Teaching of Foreign Languages (ACTFL), the development and implementation of extended sequences of well-articulated foreign language instruction in K-8 schools has been vigorous and healthy in some cases and inconsistent and unsustainable in others. The story we wish to tell is about this contrast and difference. Just as the main characters of Dickens' novel represent two contrasting personalities, Darnay, the romantic French aristocrat, and Carton, the cynical English lawyer, the story of K-8 foreign language programs is also one of passionate commitment or wavering optimism toward the inclusion of foreign language education in the school's curriculum.

This story is based on our continuing work since 1991 with two different schools that wished to implement foreign language education in the elementary grades.[1] Our work in these two schools involved collaborative planning meetings, curriculum development and longitudinal research to assess the progress that students made as they moved through the grades. What we hope to show in this educational narrative is that, although both schools aimed to provide the best world language education possible for their students, only one school produced a program that was sustainable and fully integrated into the life of the school. In the case of the other school, the program was closed two years before we began to write this story. Why this occurred, what we learned from our research and how others can learn from these two experiences is the purpose of this book.

How to read the story

Our claim in this account is not to provide the definitive formula for successful programs. As Eggington (2005) states, any language planning activity – including policies for the teaching and learning of additional languages in school districts – is embedded within a series of immediate and interconnected eco-systems. That is, one program model or set of considerations for program development cannot be applied to all school districts without careful consideration of specific local factors that influence educational change. For example, parental attitude toward language learning and their own histories as language learners, faculty support for language learning, time for instruction, the position of a program in the school curriculum and monetary resources are a few of the myriad factors that are consequential to what gets implemented, received and regularized. However, based on our experience with acquisition planning and research in the eco-systems of these two schools, we have identified prominent themes through research that form a profile of a successful program. It is our hope, therefore, that this story will offer guidance to school districts, administrators and teachers seeking to implement early foreign language learning programs (EFLLP). Where programs already exist, we hope our research will provide assistance to those who wish to assess current practices and program outcomes. We maintain that the credibility and sustainability of early language programs nationwide depend largely on serious research investigations of program practices and outcomes. Through research into programs, we can ensure consistent and sustainable quality instruction for all children in world language programs (see also Rosenbusch & Jensen, 2005; National Association of State Boards of Education, 2003).

As our story unfolds, we hope that those involved with the foreign language education of young children will be able to identify experiences that connect to their own programs or realize that our tale may contrast with theirs in whole or in part. Moreover, comparing and contrasting local experiences through the lens of the context of specific programs allows for an understanding of why programs function as they do. Thus, the generalizability of this research is not found entirely in external factors such as *all* elementary school children or *all* elementary school foreign language teachers who teach them. Rather, our research is centrally concerned with deepening our understanding of the educational activity of teaching children ages five to 13 in a foreign language in American schools. In this way, we believe that our research generalizes to the concept of early language learning programs rather than to specific groups of individuals or practices involved in these programs. Moreover, we believe that the research plan that we present in detail in later chapters can serve as a framework for research into other programs. This research framework illustrates how various aspects of a school's ecology come into play when evaluating foreign language education programs.

Why is this story important to tell?

Understanding the dynamics of early language learning programs in the local context in which they occur is important for two reasons. First, recent professional concern for the lack of advanced and superior levels of language proficiency on the part of graduates has led to the national priority of achieving stronger proficiency gains as an outcome of our programs. EFLLPs clearly play a role in addressing this priority. Second, the idiosyncratic and variable structure of foreign language teaching in the elementary school makes comparative research all the more difficult and complex. Given the lack of comparability of early language programs, making general claims about the young language learner, the level of his/her achievement and the relationship of this achievement to program characteristics is extremely difficult and highly context bound. As Hamayan (1998) has so aptly pointed out, understanding early foreign language programs and how children achieve in these programs is like painting a chameleon. Just as the animal's colors depend on its physical surroundings, any one representation becomes inaccurate as soon as this background changes. Language programs in the early grades, especially one teaching a language that is perceived as non-essential to the daily life of the community, is similarly hard to depict.

Over the past few years, many professional language organizations and regional conferences and consortiums have turned their attention to the issue of advanced and superior language proficiency. As we write this monograph, hardly a day goes by that some individual or organization does not call for the implementation of programs or innovative practices that will help to develop graduates with higher degrees of proficiency in various languages of so-called strategic importance to the USA. For example, at an international education event at the State Department in Washington, which brought together university presidents from around the country, President George W. Bush (January 5, 2008) said that the USA must promote the study of foreign cultures and languages and encourage students from overseas to attend colleges and universities here as part of the strategy against terrorism. The US government, he noted, needs diplomats, soldiers and intelligence officers who are fluent in the languages of the Muslim world in order to promote the spread of freedom and fight the battle against terrorists. Language skills are 'part of the strategic goals to protect this country'. Although one may argue with this rationale of why language should be taught and learned, it represents, nonetheless, a renewed national awareness of the importance of language proficiency as central to the education of the country's citizenry and to the strength of the nation.

The impact of political events on the language teaching profession has been significant in our history. Four decades ago, the launching of Sputnik led to a temporary growth in the number and variety of language programs. More recently, the current world political situation has led to a growth of language programs aimed to develop advanced and superior ranges of proficiency and research centers devoted exclusively to demonstrating how this goal can be achieved (e.g. the Center for Advanced Language Proficiency Education and Research (CALPER) located at Pennsylvania State University, the Center for Advanced Study of Language (CASL) at the University of Maryland and others). Despite recent initiatives to address the widespread lack of advanced and superior language outcomes of programs, it is ironic that foundational language education programs in American K-12 public education are often viewed as 'problematic, difficult, and undesirable' (Tucker, 2001). This perception is particularly applicable to foreign language education in the elementary grades where current nationally mandated testing has created the need for schools to spend the majority of their time and resources on mathematics and reading English. If foreign language learning has been perceived as difficult in the past, this scenario is even more pronounced under the current requirements for the assessment of 'basic skills'.

Thus, a major question that these current initiatives seek to answer is how can students in American schools graduate with advanced proficiency and cross-cultural competence as a matter of course in the foreseeable future? We believe that by reporting on the successes and the challenges of the programs with which we have been involved, important issues can be brought to light concerning the design of sustainable early foreign language programs and how these programs can connect to the broader professional agenda of fostering a language competent society. It is now clear that advanced level competence cannot be achieved after two years of language study in high school or at a university. Advanced and superior level proficiency require systematic study of a foreign language across several years of instruction. As our story will show, academically serious and well-designed foreign language programs in the elementary and middle school are the prerequisites to advanced and superior levels of language proficiency in later years.

We have found consistently over the years that students can make steady progress in elementary school programs that are designed with language proficiency and cultural competence as explicit goals. It is also well known that students who begin the study of a foreign language in the later years of schooling often do not surpass intermediate levels of proficiency as defined by the ACTFL (1999) proficiency guidelines. Beginning instruction in a foreign language in the early years of school increases the probability that students who continue their study will graduate from university with advanced proficiency and cross-cultural competence as a matter of course in the foreseeable future. But this scenario can only be achieved if early language learning programs provide adequate instructional time and resources, equate the importance of language learning with the learning of other academic subjects and incorporate language learning centrally into the school curriculum and into the life of the school. Our story documents these issues and describes what the pathway to advanced proficiency may look like. Conversely, our story also illustrates how this pathway may lead to a dead end under certain unfavorable conditions.

A second reason why research is needed on elementary school foreign language programs is that foreign language program models vary greatly from state to state and even within school districts, unlike other subject areas such as mathematics and English language arts. We see program variability in the myriad configurations of foreign language programs. These configurations include exploratory programs, regularly scheduled time for instruction during each school day, irregularly scheduled instructional time during the week or school year, programs beginning at different grade levels in either elementary or middle school, and even after-school programs when, for whatever reasons, time in the school day cannot be found for language instruction. Compounding this array of program models is the inconsistency across schools concerning time allocated for instruction. It is fairly well accepted that 75 minutes a week constitutes the minimum amount of time required for a *bona fide* elementary school foreign language program (Curtain & Dahlberg, 2004). But as many in this field know, the amount of time devoted to foreign language study is almost always *less* than the time given to other subject areas. Unfortunately, adjustments to the expectations of student outcomes based on time for instruction are often not considered when assessing whether a program is successful.[2] For reasons such as these, conducting research and making research claims about foreign language education in the elementary school is extremely difficult.

Due to the variability of program models, our story will focus solely on programs considered by the profession to be *bona fide* and legitimate foreign language programs for children. That is, these programs provide adequate instructional time and were not, at least initially, what some would call 'minimal courses'. Both schools made efforts to allot consistent amounts of time during the school day for foreign language instruction and the curricula were developed to reflect a proficiency-oriented, standards-based approach. The teachers were certified in foreign language teaching and, in some cases, held an additional certification in elementary education or an advanced degree in education (e.g. a master's degree in foreign language education). In other words, the schools in which we worked could be considered best-case settings for foreign language programs in the K-8 environment, based on what we know about the vast programmatic differences in how foreign language instruction is currently delivered across the country.

Essential Questions

A number of essential questions that have shaped the direction of our research in these two schools over the years motivate this story. These questions derived from previous research, our conversations with school district personnel and our observations of the two programs. As we consulted the research literature, we soon realized that studies of early language learning were relatively scant. The studies and position papers that were available often involved programs outside the USA and they needed to be read and interpreted carefully in light of the American educational context (see, e.g. Cameron, 2001; Clyne *et al.*, 1995; Genesee, 1987). In some cases, comparisons between research findings from other countries and the USA were not possible. In other cases, the particular program model precludes deriving insight from research, such as the case of immersion or dual language programs. Although other countries initiated and examined early language programs (see, for example the case of Clyne *et al.* (1995) for Australia), it was clear that naive cross-national comparison was not the best way to understand and shed light on language learning in the American elementary school context. Contextual factors, such as national consciousness for the value of language study, language education policy, the degree of bilingualism or multilingualism of the country and attitudes toward users of languages other than the national language preclude making claims from research in these contexts.

Additionally, a majority of studies concerning the young language learner in the existing research literature were restricted, for the most part, to the learning of English as a second language in American schools (see, e.g. Genesee *et al.*, 2006) or to the learning of additional languages in immersion programs, such as French in Canada (Lapkin, 1998; Johnson & Swain, 1997; Lambert, 1984). From a contextual perspective, neither of these two settings involved programs that were similar to the types of early foreign language programs that were beginning to take hold in American K-8 schools.

Because of our interactions with teachers, administrators and parents, a number of important and essential questions emerged within our particular context. These questions can be grouped into three broad categories: (1) planning program implementation, (2) monitoring and documenting program outcomes and (3) unanticipated issues and challenges. As we began detailed planning discussions with administrators and teachers at each of the two schools, particular questions emerged that were idiosyncratic to each school, an issue we will discuss later in this volume. Although the overarching themes remained the same for the two schools, how the questions emerged and were answered, and what was discovered differed considerably across the schools. These answers, as we will see later, were consequential to each program's future sustainability. The purpose of reviewing the essential questions guiding our research is to provide the rationale for how we approached our examination of these two early foreign language education programs. We will look closely at these questions and their significance, how they were answered and our findings in the later chapters of this book.

The question of language selection surfaced as a central concern early on in discussions with both schools. Following language selection, the choice of program model emerged as an important concern. Finding time in an already overcrowded school day required careful deliberation both with the schedule and with teachers – especially those in other subject areas where a sacrifice of a few minutes would have to be made. As program models took shape, assessing program outcomes within given years of instruction and across years was raised as an important issue. Here, the university partners (see Chapter 2) played an important role in working with the schools' personnel to decide what was important to assess, how to conduct these assessments, and when and by whom assessments should be carried out. Related to this matter of assessment were questions concerning how the assessment measures were to be constructed, who was to be involved in developing the instruments, how assessment results were to be used and to whom information should be communicated. Given the dearth of valid and reliable assessments for early language learners (Donato, 1998), this aspect of our work occupied a large portion of our collaborative efforts with the schools and was a prime source of information for much of what we now know concerning foreign language programs for the young learner.

Unexpected issues also surfaced in these schools, leading to an additional set of unanticipated and complex questions. As students moved through a particular program model, questions arose relative to program priorities and practices. For example, how to maintain student motivation to ensure continual language development across years of instruction was a theme that was central in both schools. Moreover, what counts as progress came into focus as an essential question. As students progressed in their comprehension and speaking skills, it became clear that assessing reading and writing development was also crucial. This was particularly true in the Spanish school where the program model shifted in the middle school grades (6–8) to content-based instruction.[3] Content-based instruction requires strong literacy skills for interpreting and producing academic language and for engaging in academic and text-based discussions. This issue led to other concerns that required questioning the time-honored assumptions about content-based or content-related instruction. That is, what does the connection look like in terms of classroom talk and text, what are the challenges when making the language and content connections, and how can teachers be assisted in understanding and carrying out content-based instruction when their training and experiences were based on traditional models of standards-based instruction. The modes of communication as specified in the National Standards for Foreign Language Learning (NSFLL) (2006) do not delineate between varying genre of language use in particular textual domains. Thus, we faced the issue of assessing clearly and differentiating between student language gains in the K-5 setting and the type of language needed when the focus of instruction shifted to language as the content and vehicle of instruction in a content-based language program.

In the context of all these questions, the teacher and those associated with the programs remained central to our investigation. School ambiance, or the attitudes, assumptions and dispositions of program constituents, was believed to influence the evolution of the program, student progress and attitudes, and school board satisfaction (Donato *et al.*, 1996). In this way, our research at these two schools yielded both quantitative data in the form of language achievement measures as well as results from attitude and opinion questionnaires, as well as qualitative data in the form of observations of classroom interactions and artifact analysis that served as an interpretive lens for understanding various aspects of student achievement and teacher practices. Taken together, these data points resulted in a comprehensive profile of a program's effectiveness, or the lack of it, and reasons for a program's success or challenges.

In the next section, we will describe the state of contemporary foreign language education in the USA and, by contrast, the state of foreign language education in other selected countries throughout the world. One purpose of this review is to highlight the relative scarcity within the USA of programs such as the ones with which we have been working.

Brief Review of US Experiences

Approximately a decade ago, federal legislation was enacted in the USA, the so-called Goals 2000: Educate America Act, that called for American students to leave grades 4, 8 and 12 having 'demonstrated competence over challenging subject matter including English, mathematics, science, [and] foreign languages'. Although *every* European country has a national policy for introducing at least one foreign language into the elementary school curriculum of every child (see, e.g. Pufahl *et al.*, 2000; Dickson & Cumming, 1996), the situation is much bleaker in the USA. Today, nearly a decade later, we are far from achieving the goal of *offering* foreign languages to every student in grades 4, 8 and 12; much less certifying that all students can demonstrate age and grade level competence in a foreign language.

Foreign language education in US schools

The Center for Applied Linguistics (CAL) and ACTFL, with support from the US Department of Education, have periodically examined the state of foreign language education in the USA. CAL has documented (in 1987, 1997 and is doing so again in 2007–2008 as this monograph is being written) the percentage of schools that offer instruction in public and private elementary schools (operationally defined in their research as comprising kindergarten through grade 8) and secondary schools (defined as grades 9 through 12). Their most recent report (Rhodes & Branaman, 1999) indicated that only 31% of American elementary schools offered any foreign language instruction at all, with approximately twice as many private schools offering foreign language instruction as public schools. Although the overall proportion of schools offering a foreign language has increased from approximately 22% in 1987 to 31% in 1997, the numbers are still woefully small. A description of the ongoing survey that is scheduled for completion in 2009 can be found at http://www.cal.org/projects/flsurvey.html.

The ACTFL association has also periodically assessed foreign language enrollments in public secondary schools. They have operationally separated their report into data for grades 7 and 8 and grades 9–12. Their most recent report (Draper & Hicks, 2002) presents some very bleak data for Fall 2000. They found that approximately seven million students were enrolled in foreign language courses in grades 7–12 in American public schools. This represented about 33.8% of the total enrollment of public secondary schools. In 1994 (the year that a previous survey had been completed), just over six million students were studying a foreign language, or just 32.8% of the total public secondary school population. In the six-year period from the time of the first survey, it is clear that the number of students studying a foreign language in public schools did not rise drastically or show signs of any sizable increase in enrollments.

At the high school level alone (grades 9–12), slightly fewer than six million students (43.8%) were studying a foreign language in 2000, an increase of approximately 2% over 1994. However, they reported that there was a drop in enrollment of approximately 2% at the junior high school (grades 7 and 8), where only 14.7% of students were enrolled in 2000 compared with 16.2% in 1994. The message in the data gathered by CAL and the ACTFL seems to be that relatively few schools offer foreign languages as subjects for study to all their students. The data indicate that foreign language programs in the elementary school are scarce, despite claims that a language competent society is a national priority. When early language learning programs do exist, relatively few districts require all students to be in foreign language classes or students opt not to take advantage of the opportunity for foreign language study.

If American students are to achieve demonstrable proficiency in a foreign language on completion of grades 4, 8 and 12, the number of programs at all levels will need to be significantly expanded and improved and significantly more students will need to be enticed or compelled to participate. This is particularly true at the elementary level. The importance of including foreign language study in elementary school is also supported by research on the amount of instructional time required for developing functional proficiency in a foreign language (Carroll, 1967). These research findings are also reflected in the widely held professional view that language competence can only be achieved by children who follow well articulated, sustained sequences of foreign language instruction (Donato & Terry, 1995; Rosenbusch & Jensen, 2005). By expanding foreign language instruction in the elementary school, students will have an extended opportunity to achieve the goals that have been widely articulated and disseminated as the National Standards for Foreign Language Education (ACTFL, 2007). They will also have an opportunity to develop a truly functional ability in a language other than their first language, the ultimate goal of foreign language instruction.

A major objection to incorporating foreign language instruction into the elementary school curriculum seems to be that there is not enough time in the instructional day (Baranick & Markham, 1986). Our present national concerns with systemic educational reform and with competitiveness make this a critical time to explore more fully the factors related to the implementation of elementary school foreign language programs. It is ironic that other countries in the world find adequate amounts of time for language study without compromising student learning in other subject areas. In fact, some of these countries outperform the USA on some achievement measures (OECD, 2005). Without oversimplifying the situation, it might be useful to make cross-national comparisons to identify ways that schools make time for additional language study and to determine if these options might be instituted in US public schools. Until the issue of time for language study in the school day is resolved, we will continue to face obstacles in implementing viable programs of study in the elementary grades that will ultimately constitute the foundation for sustained language learning in the later years of schooling. We turn our attention to this issue in the next section of the chapter.

Although the primary focus of this monograph is on foreign language study in grades K-8, it is also worth noting that the already bleak picture in the USA becomes even worse at the tertiary level. The Modern Language Association (MLA) periodically surveys colleges and universities across the country to collect enrollment data. The most recent survey (Wells, 2004) found that approximately 8.6% of tertiary students in 2002 were studying a foreign language (compared with 7.9% in 1998). That is, about 91% of our tertiary students were *not* studying an additional language.

Brief Review of International Experiences

Let's consider for a moment the situation in other countries. The number of languages spoken throughout the world is estimated to be approximately 6000 (Grimes, 1992). Although people frequently observe that a small number of languages such as Arabic, Bengali, English, French, Hindi, Malay, Mandarin, Portuguese, Russian and Spanish serve as important link languages or languages of wider communication around the world, these are very often spoken as second, third, fourth or later-acquired languages by their speakers (see, e.g. Cheshire, 1991; Comrie, 1987; Edwards, 1994). Although fewer than 25% of the world's approximately 200 countries recognize two or more official languages – with a mere handful recognizing *more than two* (e.g. India, Luxembourg, Nigeria, etc.) – available data indicate that there are many more bilingual or multilingual individuals in the world than there are monolingual. In addition, many more children throughout the world have been, and continue to be, educated via a second or a later-acquired language – at least for some portion of their formal education – than the number of children educated exclusively via their first language. In many parts of the world, bilingualism or multilingualism and innovative approaches to education that involve the use of two or more languages constitute the normal everyday experience of children (see, e.g. Dutcher, 1994; World Bank, 1995).

The use of multiple languages in education may be attributed to, or be a reflection of, numerous factors such as the linguistic heterogeneity of a country or region (e.g. Luxembourg or Singapore); specific social or religious attitudes (e.g. the addition of Sanskrit to mark Hinduism or Pali to mark Buddhism); or the desire to promote national identity (e.g. in India, Nigeria and the Philippines). More often, throughout the world, innovative language education programs are implemented to promote proficiency in international language(s) of wider communication together with proficiency in national and regional languages. In numerous countries in Asia, the Middle East and Latin America, English is being introduced to students as an additional language for study at an earlier age. For example, in Qatar, following the development of new educational standards by the Supreme Education Council, science and mathematics will be taught via English from kindergarten through grade 12 in 'public' schools throughout the country.

Selected national examples of foreign language education

In other countries, foreign or additional languages are being introduced as subjects for study in earlier grade levels. To take four examples from the recently completed study of literacy education in 40 countries around the world (Kennedy *et al.*, 2007):

Holland
Dutch is the first language of instruction in schools, although Frisian or a regional dialect also may be taught alongside Dutch. English is the first foreign language students learn, beginning in the last 3 years of primary school. (Kennedy *et al.*, 2007: 269)

Singapore
A cornerstone of Singapore's education system is the bilingual policy, which encourages children to be proficient in both English, the language of global business, commerce, and technology, and their mother-tongue, the language of their cultural heritage. English is the medium of instruction for all subjects in schools except civics and moral education and the mother-tongue languages. As a result of the bilingual education policy, the proportion of residents who are literate in two or more languages increased from 45% in 1990 to 56% in 2000. (Kennedy *et al.*, 2007: 351)

Spain
As in other European countries, the number of schools in Spain that have adopted a Content and Language Integrated Learning curriculum, in which some of the curriculum subjects are taught in English, has grown considerably in the past decade. (Kennedy *et al.*, 2007: 393)

Sweden
Swedish is the majority language in Sweden, and, therefore, is spoken in all areas of society. Everyone has the opportunity to learn Swedish, as well as a foreign language and their mother-tongue or minority language in all years of schooling. (Kennedy *et al.*, 2007: 403)

As indicated, it is not only English that is being studied as an additional language by students. As Graddol (2006) noted, for example, the study of Spanish is now compulsory in all secondary schools in Brazil. Furthermore, Graddol (1999, 2006) noted that many millions of students in countries such as India and South Korea are now studying Mandarin. In an earlier report, summarizing the pilot phase of a proposed study to be conducted of innovative language education programs and student attainment in countries throughout the world, Dickson and Cumming (1996) noted that in 23 of the 25 countries surveyed, it was the norm for all children to study at least one and often two or three additional languages as part of the compulsory cycle of education. The two 'outliers' were England and the USA that did *not* require foreign language study.

A cross-national perspective: The case of England and the USA

To illustrate further the differences in the priority that countries assign to early foreign language learning in schools, we will examine recent initiatives in England compared to the recent state of elementary school foreign language programs in the USA. We begin the analysis with a summary of the recent CAL survey entitled *Foreign Language Teaching in U.S. Schools*, published in 2010 (Rhodes & Pufahl, 2010). We follow with an overview of England's National Language Strategy called 'Languages for All: Languages for Life – A Strategy for England'. We will conclude our comparative analysis with reasons why early foreign language learning policy differs so radically across nations and how, in the chapters that follow, our longitudinal study might inform programs both here and abroad.

Many school districts in the USA that have previously boasted sequential programs beginning in the early years of elementary school are finding that their programs are being scaled down, that particular grade levels are being eliminated from the instructional sequence or that time for instruction is being dramatically reduced. The recent *CAL National Survey of Foreign Language Teaching in U.S. Schools* reports that the percentage of public elementary and middle schools offering foreign language instruction decreased significantly from 1997 to 2008: from 31 to 25% of all public elementary schools and from 75 to 58% of all middle schools. It is important to note, however, that this disheartening picture of early language learning is not representative of the past several decades. The CAL survey also points out that from 1987 to 1997, EFLLPs were on the rise with a documented increase from 22 to 31% of elementary schools offering language instruction in the elementary grades. French programs accounted for 41% of elementary language programs and German programs accounted for 10%. After making important progress over a 10-year period between 1987 and 1997, the USA has declined significantly in its commitment to providing foreign language instruction to young children. In 2008, only 25% of elementary schools have been reported to offer foreign language instruction. This sharp decrease has occurred primarily in the public school system. The percentage of private schools offering a foreign language to young learners has remained relatively unchanged, with a difference of only two percentage points between 1997 (53%) and 2008 (51%). In contrast to private schools, 24% of public elementary schools offered a foreign language in 1997 compared to 15% of these schools that sustained programs in 2008. The survey also found that the most dramatic decreases in programs occurred in rural schools with a decline from 25 to 16%. Clearly, the recent profile of early language learning in the USA is not an optimistic one and appears to suggest that foreign language learning is not among the national priorities for educating the nation's youth. As high-stakes state and national testing of English, reading and mathematics becomes more extensive in US public schools, districts have been forced to pay closer attention to these subject areas. Districts have opted to increase the time allotted to instruction in areas most commonly tested and, as a result, to reduce time for instruction, or entire programs, that are not directly connected to the contents of high-stakes tests. It comes as no surprise that foreign language programs have been seriously affected, as documented in the CAL survey. Foreign languages are not part of the state and national assessment initiatives and student performance in languages other than English is not considered a strength of a school district's instructional program (see Chapter 3 for more on the culture of assessment and its effects on foreign language programs).

In contrast to the decline of early foreign language programs in the USA, England presents a mirror image of program growth over the years. From the 1960s, England and Wales have paid serious attention to national language needs through a commitment to investigating the advantages of an early start. Called the Pilot Scheme (Rowlands, 1972), the longest investigation of early language learning was conducted in Britain (from 1963 to 1973) to determine the advantages and challenges of beginning foreign language instruction in French starting at age eight compared to the traditional sequence of beginning instruction in high school. Findings from this 10-year longitudinal study indicate that the picture of early language learning programs in Britain diverges dramatically from the ebbs and flows of program research and development in the USA. Rowlands (1972) states that the development of foreign language teaching in primary school initially followed patterns similar to those in the USA. However, Rowlands (1972: 13) goes on to observe that 'the subsequent stages of this development have been quite different. Whereas the majority of the United States FLES programs seem to have collapsed, frequently in disillusion and disarray, [here] in Britain, French is now and established part of the curriculum of some 30-35 percent of the primary schools, and is, as far as one can judge, continuing to spread'.

In her discussion of early language learning in England, Davin (2010) presents a succinct summary of the most recent initiatives within the past decade and states that during the past 10 years, England has continued to make important changes and improvements to early language learning. After several years of development, in 2001 the Council of Europe published the Common European Framework of Reference for Languages (CEFR). The CEFR framework outlines a comprehensive description of foreign language knowledge and skills in several communicative domains and, in so doing, has created a standard of reference for foreign language education throughout the continent and provided an impetus for change in language education. The year following the publication of the CEFR, the European Council called for further action in the field of foreign language education. They stated that further action should be taken:

> to improve the mastery of basic skills, in particular by teaching at least two foreign languages from a very early age: establishment of a linguistic competence indicator in 2003; development of digital literacy: generalisation of an Internet and computer user's certificate for secondary school pupils. (European Council, 2002: 19)

Soon after this declaration, the Department of Education and Skills (DfES) published the National Languages Strategy, called 'Languages for All: Languages for Life – A Strategy for England'. This report described the importance of learning languages and outlined the government's vision of foreign language learning and key objectives that should be included in all programs. One of the three main goals of this report was to introduce foreign language learning to all students in Key Stage 2 (KS2) by 2010. KS2 refers to students in their 3rd, 4th, 5th and 6th years of school, or children between the ages of 7 and 11. This strategy stated that all children should have the opportunity to reach a recognized level of proficiency by age 11 (DfES, 2002).

Since the National Languages Strategy was published, the number of early language learning programs in England has steadily increased. In 2009, the National Foundation for Educational Research (NFER) published results of a three-year longitudinal study of language learning at KS2. In 2006, 2007 and 2008, the NFER surveyed a representative sample of 500 primary schools and found that in 2008, 92% of primary schools were offering foreign language classes to students in some but not all of the target KS2 grade levels. Although not every school had succeeded in offering foreign language classes to the four KS2 grade levels, 69% of these schools were found to have instituted foreign language classes for all four years of KS2. Further results of the survey indicate that only about 18% of schools will not be able to provide language learning for all four years of KS2 by 2010, and that by 2011 it is expected that language education in England will become a statutory requirement (Wade et al., 2009). While this may be cause for concern in Britain, here in the USA the percentage is much higher with 75% of elementary schools not providing foreign language instruction in any form.

Whereas the National Languages Strategy caused widespread reform all over England (Wade et al., 2009), in the USA, action from the government has not had such profound effects. In 2004, the US Department of Defense and the Center for Advanced Study of Language held the National Language Conference. The result of this conference was a publication entitled *A Call to Action for National Foreign Language Capabilities* (2005), which called for better foreign language education for all students, and in 2006, the National Security Language Initiative was instituted to increase funding for early language learning. Yet, despite these positive steps to expand language instruction in schools and increase national language competence, the number of early language learning programs has continued to decline. As schools struggle to cope with national assessments in mathematics and reading, resources are scarce for early language learning programs and attention is focused on these high-stakes subjects (Rhodes & Pufahl, 2010).

The purpose of this volume is to investigate how these declines occur in some schools and to compare shrinking programs to those that are developed and implemented and sustain themselves over time. In comparing the history of early language learning in England to that in the USA, it is clear that national initiatives produce differential effects. Whereas in England, the call to action produced increases in foreign language programs across the grade levels, the response to national initiatives in the USA seems to have been derailed by competing educational priorities. National educational policy, such as No Child Left Behind, and the skeptical, if not negative, attitudes toward foreign language learning among some school administrators and parents have prevented the expansion of foreign language programs even when presented with possibilities to begin expanding programs in the early grades of elementary school.

An overview of international foreign language education

The composite portrait of language education policies and practices throughout the world is exceedingly complex – and simultaneously fascinating. In Eritrea, for instance, an educated person will likely have attended some portion of schooling taught via Tigrinya *and* Arabic *and* English – and developed proficiency in reading these languages, which are written using three different scripts (Ge'ez, Arabic and Roman). In Oceania, to take a different example, linguists estimate that a mere 4% of the world's population speaks approximately 20% of the world's 6000 languages. In Papua New Guinea, a country that has a population of approximately 3 million, linguists have described more than 870 languages (Summer Institute of Linguistics, 1995). Here it is common for a child to grow up speaking one local indigenous language at home, another in the market place, adding Tok Pisin to his/her repertoire as a lingua franca, and English if he/she continues his/her schooling. Analogous situations recur in many parts of the world, such as India, which has declared 15 of its approximately 1650 indigenous languages to be 'official'.

One might ask why has the USA become such an outlier with respect to the study of foreign or second languages as part of our national program of education. What can be done to encourage and assist school districts to introduce the study of an additional language as part of the so-called core curriculum? These are among the questions that we propose to explore in this monograph.

Notes

1. In this monograph, we refer to the schools as the Japanese school or the Japanese program and the Spanish school or the Spanish program since these are the areas of interest in our study and the extent of our research and collaboration with the school districts. Additionally, we refer to the programs as early foreign language learning programs (EFLLP) rather than foreign language in the elementary school (FLES) or foreign language exploratory (FLEX). Our reason for this designation is to avoid assigning one or other model to these programs, which emerged and took shape as the programs were implemented and assessed.
2. The ACTFL Performance Guidelines for K-12 Learners (American Council on Teaching of Foreign Languages, 1998) is one attempt at codifying outcomes based on years of study and start time.
3. Although the school refers to its curriculum as content-based, in practice, lessons are based on (1) academic content that is already taught in other subject areas and (2) extensions of the academic content into topics that are connected to the Spanish language and cultures, e.g. analyzing Mayan civilizations. For this reason, we think this program is best described

as a combination of content-related and content-based foreign language instruction. Additionally, the foreign language teachers find themselves at times introducing academic content in advance of the subject area teachers. The dichotomous distinction between content-based and content-related becomes impossible in actual programs where the coordination of content teaching in the foreign language class with instruction in the adjacent academic subject area is fluid and subject to the typical changes in schedule and pace of student learning.

Chapter 2
Program Development and Implementation: A Contrastive Story

In this chapter, we will describe the two sites that we have been working with since 1992. We have been fortunate to be 'invited in' to participate in the lives of these schools over the past 15 years. With their permission, we have described the programs; but we have preserved the anonymity of the participating students, parents and teachers. For this reason, and as stated in the first chapter, we will refer to these schools as the Japanese school and the Spanish school. Where it is entirely clear that the section of the chapter refers to either the Japanese program or the Spanish program, we will simply refer to each site as 'the school' or 'the program'. Likewise, in any of the public presentations that we have made over the years to parents, teachers, administrators or professional colleagues, we have carefully preserved the confidentiality of those whom we tested, interviewed, observed or from whom we collected questionnaire information.

The Japanese Program: 1992–2005

The first program that we began intensive work on was the Japanese program. The school, established in 1931 as a laboratory school, offers instruction from kindergarten through grade 8. According to its mission statement, the school is built on four cornerstones: *community, creativity, inquiry* and *freedom*. The school's approximately 300 students reflect the diversity of the greater urban area in which it is located – approximately 7% are European-American, 9% African-American and 14% Asian-American or other minorities. The school provides multi-age classrooms, modified team teaching and non-graded instruction for children, focused around three curricular areas – science, mathematics and the language arts. The school conceives of itself as a center of inquiry whose mission is to generate new knowledge about teaching, to support the intellectual growth of teachers and to develop an inquiring attitude in students.

The origins of the K-8 Japanese program

In the fall of 1991, the executive committee of the school decided to examine its curriculum and ask some hard questions. What was unique about the school and how was the school keeping pace with the new demands of preparing students to live in a global society? The Japanese school had always been proud of its reputation in the community as an innovative inquiry-based K-8 school. Yet, schools can all too often become complacent and rely on their reputation rather than on continuing self-examination. As a result of deliberations, the committee decided that the school needed to review its curriculum and, in the words of the chair, find 'something unique and special about the school', which would once again place the school in a position of prominence in the community and the nation.

In the early 1990s, the economies of the countries of the Pacific Rim (e.g. Japan, Korea, and Taiwan) were booming, with growth in their gross domestic products (GDP) regularly surpassing that of the USA. Imports of East Asian goods to the USA regularly exceeded exports from the USA, which rapidly shifted the balance of trade. The political situation in each of these countries was relatively stable, the workforce was well educated and wages were relatively low compared to the USA. Given these conditions, and the growing concern about a global economy, improving on and expanding the foreign language and culture curriculum was selected as the target of change for the school.

During academic year 1991–1992, an exploratory French and Spanish program was offered to all students in grade 6 followed by student selection of either French or Spanish for a two-level sequence of study in grades 7 and 8. Following their deliberations, the executive committee made the decision to expand foreign language study to the elementary school (K-5) and that Japanese would be the foreign language of study by all students. At the time, Japanese was a so-called less commonly taught language in the USA, a situation that is no longer true today (as an example, Japanese was reported to be studied by 1746 students at college level in 1960 and by 66,605 in 2006; see Furman *et al.*, 2007) and elementary schools typically did not offer foreign language programs in their K-5 curriculum (only 22% offered foreign language instruction in any language in 1987 with Japanese accounting for less than one tenth of 1%; see Branaman & Rhodes, 1998). Thus, from the perspective of the executive committee, uniqueness could be achieved through the implementation of an innovative Japanese program in the K-5 curriculum.

Planning the program

Because the Japanese school was connected to the graduate school of education of a large research university, the executive committee turned to the foreign language education faculty to develop the new K-5 program. All responsibility for curriculum development and teacher selection was given to the program coordinator of foreign language education, who saw this initiative as an opportunity to become involved in the life of the laboratory school and to develop potential research opportunities. During the 1991-1992 academic year, a search was conducted for a teacher. Because Japanese was not a foreign language included for licensure by the state of Pennsylvania, finding a Japanese teacher involved a process of locating a person who had native or near-native-like proficiency in the language, a comprehensive knowledge of the culture and a background in teaching young children. As new strategically important languages enter the curriculum (as is the case with Chinese and Arabic at the time of this publication), locating and hiring qualified teachers often lag behind program implementation. For this reason, it was not expected that a highly qualified foreign language teacher would be located; currently defined as a graduate of a state-approved comprehensive teacher certification program. Rather, we opted to find someone with a degree in education and experience working with young children. The first teacher hired in the Japanese school was a recent graduate of a local university who was a native speaker of Japanese, had received a master's degree in education and held an instructional certificate in elementary education. By working with the program coordinator of foreign language education on the curriculum the summer before the Japanese program was implemented, it was assumed that foreign language specific pedagogical skills and knowledge would be developed.

After the teacher had been hired, curriculum development began during the year (1991-1992) before the opening of the program. The first-year curriculum was developed by the coordinator of foreign language education from the school of education in collaboration with the newly hired teacher. Decisions concerning time for instruction and scheduling of the K-5 classes into the school day were made with the director of the school in consultation with the foreign language education program coordinator. The group decided that the Japanese program would begin in September 1992 and would be offered to *all* children in kindergarten through grade 5. The Japanese foreign language (JFL) program adhered to the criteria of typical foreign language in the elementary school

(FLES) programs – five 15-minute classes each day totaling 75 minutes of instruction each week (Curtain & Dahlberg, 2004). At the time, this JFL program differed from other early language learning program models by its use of daily instruction rather than full-period classes over fewer days of the school week or as an after-school program. The curriculum reflected a proficiency orientation with attempts at content enrichment where appropriate and possible.

Each lesson or set of lessons focused on a theme in a context, a language function associated with the context, and some attention to grammatical or syntactic structure necessary for carrying out the specified function (Omaggio, 1993; Shrum & Glisan, 2009). During the first year of the program (1992–1993), lessons also emphasized listening comprehension over the productive skills, although students were not discouraged from using the language when production arose spontaneously in class, as is often observed in young children learning a new language. Typical during this time of burgeoning FLES programs, the emphasis was on comprehension before production and attention to the development of receptive skills rather than production of speech and writing. During the first year, children received significant amounts of Japanese input from their teacher and were systematically required to demonstrate comprehension through a number of total physical response (Asher, 2000) lessons. Production, although not neglected, was not deemed central to the children's initial contact with Japanese. When speaking was the objective of the lesson, production was limited to new lexical items, formulaic expressions for carrying out functional objectives (e.g. greeting, leave taking, stating one's address or age, etc.) and some creative, personalized responses to questions (e.g. 'What's your favorite color?').

Since the program began before the development of the national standards by the American Council on the Teaching of Foreign Languages (ACTFL), the curriculum and program were considered innovative for several reasons.[1] First, classes were offered daily rather than for a limited number of days during the week or as part of an after-school program. Second, proficiency in the language and culture was the goal of the program rather than the exploration of several languages and cultures during one academic year (Lipton, 1998), intended to lead students to a choice for 'serious language study' in later years. Third, all children in kindergarten through grade 5 participated in the program, making foreign language a required subject rather than an elective one. Finally, unlike most educational innovations at the time, longitudinal research was planned from the beginning as a way to monitor the program and the progress of the pupils. We now turn to the genesis of this aspect of the project and, in particular, the partnership of two local universities and the school that made this research a reality.

University-school partnership

During the 1991–1992 planning year of the program, the program coordinator of foreign language education had an informal discussion with a colleague at a neighboring university about plans for the Japanese program. Enticed by the idea that an elementary school foreign language program in Japanese would provide valuable information on how young children learn additional languages, specifically a non-cognate language for English-speaking children, a series of meetings was conducted between these two universities. These conversations led to a unique partnership involving personnel in the school, the Japanese program, the Japanese teacher and two major research universities in the area. Concurrent with planning the curriculum and decisions concerning the logistics of offering a new subject area in an already crowded school day, the decision was made by the two universities to forge a professional relationship to systematically monitor program implementation and student learning. This initial informal conversation led to a productive and sustained research relationship and eventually to the formation of the Early Language Learning Research Team (ELLRT) composed of Donato and Tucker and a rotating group of masters and doctoral students in foreign language education and second language acquisition from the University of Pittsburgh and Carnegie Mellon. As our story will show, the work of the team was not restricted to the Japanese program. Based on the work in the program and the reputation of the program in the community, the team was invited to enter into a partnership with another large school district in the area. We now turn to the genesis of the Spanish program in this second school.

The Spanish Program: 1995–Present

In this section, we turn our attention to the second major program that we have worked on over the years – the Spanish program. In May 1995, we were invited to attend an informal meeting with the superintendent of schools of a suburban school district and several of his key administrative staff. The invitation resulted, in part, from our previous research evaluating the diverse aspects of the implementation of a Japanese program at the elementary school (see, e.g. Donato et al., 1996; Tucker et al., 1996), and partly from the fact that Donato directs the major graduate foreign language education teacher preparation program in the region. This meeting was the beginning of a mutually beneficial and thoroughly enjoyable school district-university partnership that continues to the present day.

The school district's superintendent in 1995, opened the meeting by articulating a vision for his students and for his district – a vision that included doing something different, something daring. He proposed that a new program be developed so that all of the district's students would study a common foreign language throughout their entire scholastic career. He described clearly how American secondary school graduates in the 21st century will be competing for positions in which numeracy, literacy, problem solving and communication skills will be increasingly valued and, moreover, how he believed that students with bilingual language proficiency and cross-cultural competence will possess a comparative advantage relative to their monolingual English-speaking counterparts. He predicted that tomorrow's graduates will be forced to compete for positions in Beijing, Buenos Aires, Paris and Tokyo, not only for jobs in Baltimore, Chicago, Detroit and New York. Neither a highly proficient speaker of a foreign language nor an individual who has formally studied a foreign language, the superintendent represented what we eventually came to understand as a critically important aspect of support for this program. That is, although administrators and teachers were far from foreign language teaching specialists or users of foreign languages, they behaved and talked 'as if' foreign language was an important part of their lives. This ability to place oneself in an imagined world of multilingualism was one reason for the enormous support and enthusiasm for the program and for the eventual behavioral commitment on the part of the teachers to embrace the learning of some Spanish to keep pace with their students.

The impetus for the Spanish program

The school district in southwestern Pennsylvania is located approximately six miles or about a 20-minute drive from downtown Pittsburgh. The system, a relatively small one comprising approximately 3450 students who come from mostly European-American, working-class families, is fairly typical of the 501 districts that collectively form the Pennsylvania Department of Education. In these districts, student enrollments range from 267 to 214,288, while the number of schools operated in the school districts ranges from 1 to 264.

A number of questions were raised at our initial meeting. Was the superintendent's vision plausible? If so, in which language(s) should instruction be offered? Were there teachers available? Would the community support such a program? Would the members of the school board support such a program – and provide the necessary budgetary authorization? How could the school district and the two research universities work collaboratively to their mutual benefit?

The group decided to form an 'Elementary Foreign Language Steering Committee' to oversee the planning and implementation of the new and innovative foreign language program. Committee members consisted of the director of curriculum who chaired the group, the superintendent, principals from the elementary and the intermediate schools, selected elementary school teachers, the chair of the secondary school foreign language department and the university collaborators, including a doctoral student in foreign language education. During the early stages, the group met approximately quarterly to plan, review accomplishments and make decisions concerning priorities for future work. As appropriate, subgroups or individuals carried out specific activities, about which they reported back to the steering committee.

What language(s) were selected?

One of the first issues confronting the group was choice of language(s). A number of options were considered, including French, German, Japanese and Spanish. At the time, the district offered French, German and Spanish instruction to students in grades 9–12 on an elective basis. In addition, members of the university partnership proposed that Japanese be considered because of their work with a local innovative program, which was described earlier in this chapter. A number of factors were considered, such as the likely availability of prospective teachers and materials, potential community support and utility of proficiency in the target language for graduates.

For pragmatic reasons, the decision was made to select one language only, and to make its study compulsory for all children in grades K-5 with a view to expanding the program to a sequential and well-articulated K-12 program. At this point, the steering committee decided that it would be useful to conduct a community survey to ascertain the level of support for the program and to obtain feedback concerning the choice of language. A survey instrument was developed, piloted, revised and administered by a committee member to a sample of school district parents as well as to all members of the school board. The instrument asked parents and community members to make a rank-ordered selection of the languages to be taught, to comment on their attitude toward the implementation of foreign language study in the elementary grades and to express their willingness to assist if they should happen to know the language that would be eventually selected.

The results revealed broad general support for an innovative foreign language education program for the district and support specifically for the teaching of Spanish. It was surprising that Spanish was selected by the community given that the community reflected a strong German heritage and that a major international German corporation was located within the school district. Furthermore, the respondents indicated overwhelmingly that this new program should have the goals of developing cultural knowledge (93%) and of engaging students in the excitement of language learning (80%), and somewhat less strongly in the building of basic language proficiency (19%). This rank ordering of program priorities, as will be discussed later, was consistent with the parents' views of the Japanese program. That is, language proficiency seemed not to be a priority goal for parents for speculative reasons that will be discussed later.

At what level was the program introduced?

The second major issue that the committee discussed was whether to begin the program from the *bottom up*, that is at the kindergarten level; from the *top down*, that is working backward a year at a time from grade 9 where instruction then began; or from *both ends to meet in the middle*. After much discussion that centered on issues such as scheduling, likely teacher availability and the necessity of ensuring long-term articulation, the decision was made to propose to the school board the implementation of a Spanish FLES program to begin in September 1996 for all kindergarten children in the district. The board of school directors formally approved a motion in April 1996 to begin a Spanish FLES program for all entering kindergarten in September 1996 and to extend this program to grade 1 in September 1997 and to grade 2 in September 1998 with the systematic introduction of new cohorts of kindergarten youngsters each fall. Furthermore, the board looked to the university partners to assist with curriculum planning and with formative and summative assessment so that a decision could be made in spring 1999 whether to continue and further extend the program. With this plan, the district will have a fully articulated foreign language program from kindergarten through grade 12 in 2008–2009.

It is noteworthy that since the time of the inception of the Spanish program, it is rather common knowledge among program developers that the bottom-up approach to implementation is the best way to begin strong programs and ensure careful articulation as each year of foreign language instruction is added to the school's curriculum (Curtain & Dahlberg, 2004).

Development of an action plan

After deciding on the target language (Spanish) and the model for implementation (bottom up), the committee next turned its attention to developing an action plan. This plan outlined the essential steps and activities that would need to be addressed to ensure successful implementation the following year. Among the important items that were included in the action plan were recruiting an appropriate teacher, planning the curriculum, disseminating information about the program to the community and orienting other teachers and administrators working in the system to the development of this new program. These activities continued during late winter and spring of 1996.

At the time, the school district had one consolidated primary school building, housing grades K through 5 with 11 sections or classes of kindergarten children. A major benchmark was the hiring of the first kindergarten Spanish teacher, who was a graduate from the University of Pittsburgh with dual certification in Elementary Education and Spanish. This hiring of an applicant with dual certification became the model for the district in subsequent years. The hiring of the Spanish teacher in early summer 1996 meant that she was able to devote a substantial block of time to curriculum development activities preceding the start of the program. She worked with other curriculum specialists in the district and in continuing consultation with university collaborators. Curriculum development activities benefited from and reflected work that had been done on the ACTFL National Standards (1999, 2006) as well as innovative work that had been completed in the school district on Standards in the Arts. The Arts Standards played an important role for two reasons. First, the principal of the intermediate school (grades 3–5) was a former art teacher who maintained strong ties with her national professional organization. Second, based on her history with integrating art into the essential questions guiding the thematic planning of the elementary school curriculum, the principal saw a similar process of integrating Spanish into the already established curriculum. In this way, Spanish was mapped on the existing elementary school curriculum and integrated as an equally important component supporting the essential questions and themes in the elementary school.

How Did the Program Begin?

The Spanish program began in September 1996 with 11 classes comprising a total enrollment of 223 kindergarten students. Each class met for 20 minutes per day, five days a week – a model that continues to this day for the classes from kindergarten through grade 5. The Spanish language teaching specialists at each grade level go to the students in their regular classrooms, and in most cases, team teach with the regular classroom teacher. Growing spontaneously from the enthusiasm for the program, a strong collaboration between the classroom teachers and the Spanish language teaching specialists developed and continues to mark this program as unique (see Donato *et al.*, 1994, concerning the problem of marginality of early foreign language learning programs). Rather than expressing indifference toward the new program by neither working to support it nor repudiate it, the kindergarten teacher initially, and others through the subsequent years, have established close contact with the language teachers and freely shared materials during the curriculum development phase of the program. Additionally, grade-level and subject area teachers studied Spanish during many of the Spanish lessons in their classrooms. The Spanish program and the foreign language teachers were clearly positioned from inception as an integrated part of each grade's program and as equal participants in the total school curriculum. We will return to this point in the last chapter as an important defining factor in establishing sustainable programs that withstand the test of time and politically and financially motivated decisions to institute language study where none has previously been offered.

Curriculum development and program continuation at the early grades

The curriculum for the early grades (K-5) was initially developed following the school district's template for planned courses of study. That is, each thematically organized unit (e.g. colors and shapes, numbers, greetings, calendar and weather, clothing and body parts, fiesta and foods, etc.) was specified according to: (a) student learning outcome; (b) content, materials and activities; and (c) procedures for assessment. The main focus of each lesson was on vocabulary building and comprehension rather than production. The curriculum reflected this orientation in its assessment procedures as well as including such activities as coloring, cooking, movement activities and the playing of games. Every attempt was and continues to be made to integrate Spanish with ongoing activities in art, music, library, physical education and the computer curriculum. The integrated nature of the Spanish class is explicit and obvious in the curriculum. Children learn numbers by accompanying jumping jack calisthenics with counting, listen to age-appropriate fairy tales in Spanish, and learn days of the week in Spanish when learning them in their regular classes. The teachers use Spanish as much as possible in the classroom for instruction and classroom management, and outside the classroom to communicate with students in the hallways. They make extensive use of manipulatives and visuals and include a wide variety of authentic materials. Classes are enriched with visits by Spanish speakers and through a partnership begun in collaboration with students studying Spanish at secondary level. For example, the FLORES program – Foreign Language On Request in Elementary School – was a program designed to allow an elementary school Spanish teacher to request classes on specific topics to be taught by advanced high school students of Spanish. The high school Spanish teacher worked with students to design age-appropriate lessons in preparation for a one class period visit to an elementary school Spanish classroom where a small number of high school students would take charge of instruction for the day.

In the primary (K-2) and intermediate (3–5) grades, there are 10–11 sections per grade. The total number of students per grade has been approximately 225–250, with about 24 students per classroom. The presence of students of Hispanic background is very small with perhaps one or two Hispanic descendant students per grade. In grades K-5, six teachers are responsible for delivering Spanish instruction, one per level. This practice changes in grade 6, when two teachers teach Spanish, a model that is also followed in grades 7 and 8. In grades K-5, Spanish is taught for 20 minutes a day, five days per week, while in the sixth grade the time doubles to 40 minutes a day, five days per week. Thus, one of the goals of the K-5 program is to prepare the students to be able to participate in a more academically oriented, content-based program at grade 6 (for more information about the intentional infusion of literacy initiatives in the primary and intermediate grades, see Dominguez et al., 2005). At this middle school level, Spanish equals in importance, and in allocation of time, the other 'core' subjects such as reading, English, math, science and social studies. By contrast, in grades K-5, Spanish is considered a 'special' course together with computers, library, music and gymnastics.

In summary, between 1996 and 2001, the Spanish program continued to expand upward one grade per year. From kindergarten through grade 5, Spanish classes are offered to all children for 20 minutes per day, five days per week. All the Spanish teachers are certified in foreign language teaching and many hold dual certification in foreign language and elementary education. The K-5 curriculum is linked to the elementary school's major interdisciplinary themes and was written by the Spanish teachers in collaboration with the elementary school teachers one year before implementation.

Curriculum development and program continuation at the later grades

When the program expanded to the middle school (grade 6) in the fall of 2002, a different curricular model was adopted. Best described as content-related instruction, the grade 6–8 Spanish curricula use academic subject matter as both the content of daily lessons *and* the vehicle by which Spanish oral and written literacy is learned. The content-related curriculum was developed based on selected topics introduced in four academic subject areas of the middle school program – English/ language arts, reading, science and social studies. In collaboration with the academic subject teachers, the middle school Spanish teachers developed the Spanish curriculum by selecting major concepts (e.g. figures of speech, natural resources and the characteristics of civilizations) from each academic subject. Between 2002 and 2008, each subject area was taught in the Spanish classes for 40 minutes a day, five days a week in four nine-week units of study that rotated through the four main academic subject areas (for additional information about the program at the middle school level, see Pessoa *et al.*, 2007).

What was the role of the university partners?

Since 1995, and continuing to the time of writing (summer 2008), Donato and Tucker have continued to serve as resources to the school district. They have assisted in multiple ways – by actively participating as members of the district's Foreign Language Program Committee and by sharing information about standards-based language teaching with teachers, administrators, members of the school board and parents. They have worked with the teachers collaboratively to develop a series of end-of-year assessment procedures that have been used to monitor the students' growth and to provide formative feedback to the teachers and administrators. They have encouraged school district administrators to tell the story of the Spanish program to diverse audiences (see, e.g. Gori, 2002) and have collaborated with a school district principal on collaborative research (see, e.g. Sapienza *et al.*, 2006). They have encouraged and assisted with the substantive participation of district teachers in the Pennsylvania State Modern Language Association (PSMLA) annual convention (see, e.g. Reitlinger & Foster, 2006).

Over the years, a number of Donato and Tucker's students have completed or are currently carrying out dissertation research or have conducted research in the district (see, e.g. Dominguez, 2003a, 2003b, 2004; Hendry, in progress); while Donato and Tucker have also spoken and written widely about the district's innovative foreign language program. In all respects, they have been full and equal partners in this undertaking. This partnership is one feature that marks this venture as unique and visionary, particularly when viewed from the perspective of history and current university-school district collaborations sponsored by local consortium and grant-related projects such as Title VI and Fulbright-Hayes (see International Education and Foreign Languages: Keys to Securing America's Future, 2007). We will return to this issue in the conclusion and argue that sustainable programs require collaborative efforts in which each member benefits from the professional linkages.

Note

1. In addition to the insights gained through our work in these two schools, this account also provides a unique historical perspective on how elementary school foreign language programs developed and evolved over time based on nationally important professional initiatives concerning curriculum, standards and assessment.

Chapter 3
A Comprehensive Model of Program Evaluation

The 'culture of assessment' is a term widely used to conceptualize and redefine the success or failure of educational programs largely based on single administrations of standardized tests at prescribed times during a student's schooling. At the insistence of the federal government and through the authorization of the No Child Left Behind Act of 2001 (PL 101–110), schools today are faced with a responsibility to demonstrate student achievement and so-called 'adequate yearly progress' on a limited set of measures in English and mathematics or face a series of penalties, such as loss of funds, seizure of their programs by test-prep businesses or even closure.

In a moving narrative to a young teacher, Jonathan Kozol (2007) explores the repercussions of current views and trends on assessment. He observes that the current culture of assessment, as defined by the federal government, has created an atmosphere of high anxiety in schools, distortions and content reduction of the curriculum, and unequal educational opportunities between schools in affluent suburbs and inner-city areas. In the former schools, students come prepared to perform well on discrete point measures of learning, and schools build on this preparation thereby strengthening the already strong resources that they can offer students. In the case of what Kozol refers to as 'congenitally under funded low-performing schools' with a history of high rates of failure, the schools run the risk of further deterioration of the few resources that do exist and end up with even less.

Added to this scenario of the educationally rich getting richer and the educationally poor getting poorer are the curricular consequences of assessment practices that are disjointed from school-based concerns of teaching and learning. Because standardized assessments are reductively defined and limited in scope, a child's education is no longer viewed as a broadening of experience, knowledge and skill through the teaching of an array of subject matter that prepares students for participation in the global community of the 21st century. As worry over test results mount, school districts have gone to great lengths to prepare students for the demands of high-stakes testing. Previously rich courses of study in the arts, social studies and the sciences, once believed to be critical components of solid, well-rounded education, have ceased to be offered in many elementary schools across the nation. It is believed that cleansing the curriculum of these perceived non-essential subjects will provide additional time for teachers to prepare students in 'the basics', defined as what students need to know to score well on federally mandated tests and to save schools from federal sanctions. It is not uncommon to learn of schools offering double periods of instruction in mathematics and reading, canceling recess time and instituting after school and weekend programs to drill students on prospective test items.

The Culture of Assessment and Foreign Language Education Programs

Foreign language programs in elementary schools have also suffered from this culture of assessment policies. Historically, foreign language education has not been valued in ways similar to traditional subject areas, such as reading in English and mathematics (Reagan & Osborne, 2002). Although there has been no public disapproval of foreign language learning for all children, opposition is implied in the form of skepticism and doubt about the usefulness of offering additional languages to children. These tacit oppositions range from personal anecdotes (e.g. 'I've never learned a foreign language so why does my child have to learn one') to uninformed personal theories of how children learn (e.g. 'the child struggles with English therefore why burden the child with an additional language' or 'learning a foreign language will interfere with the development of other first language literacy skills'). In the frenetic atmosphere of preparing children to demonstrate proficiency in a limited range of skills on standardized testing, it comes as no surprise that foreign language programs that proliferated in the 1990s and early 2000s, have been targeted for closure or drastic reductions in instructional time. Unlike Shohamy's (1993) classic work on the positive effects of testing on instruction, which she called the 'backwash effect', testing and assessment today has interfered negatively with educational opportunities for many children. Insistence on strong performance on paper-and-pencil snapshot assessments has reduced learning to narrow ranges of prescribed knowledge in limited domains and predetermined skills.

Profiles of Success: Our Emerging Assessment Plan

Evaluating and assessing student success in the Japanese and Spanish programs became a key component in our work in these schools. We view assessment as ways to document what children know and can do rather than what they cannot do. In this way, our assessment plan differed significantly from standardized testing with its emphasis on past achievement rather than on gathering information on how students grow and develop over time. Additionally, as we will show, our assessment plan included various data points, including classroom observations, interviews, school climate and analysis of teaching as a discursive process. Where possible, we mapped qualitative assessments onto end-of-year quantitative measures. Data from all assessments led to curricular modifications to ensure that student progress would be steady and continual across the years. In this way, the results of our assessment plan promoted the continued study of the foreign language and program expansion rather than creating anxiety, reductions in instruction or distorted notions about children's performance in their new language. We were acutely aware that without careful assessment of all aspects of these innovative programs, progress in student learning, support from a wide range of school constituents and program credibility would probably not be achieved.

The Challenges of Conducting EFLL Research

Meaningful research on early foreign language learning (EFLL) has proven difficult to conduct in the USA. Two factors seem to have been largely responsible. First, the availability of reliable and valid instruments for assessing novice-level language performance in young children is limited. Second, there is an inherent difficulty in measuring foreign language abilities, attitudes and attitude change in young respondents. For example, we noted that young children often do not recall previous years of study, making attitude comparisons about their language learning experiences from year to year difficult and unreliable. We also found that on oral assessments, children required a gentle approach and creative ways to assess how far the child's speaking ability could be stretched. Although most probably true for adults, we found that children could reveal abilities in the target language if the interview process was not confounded by the use of the foreign language by the assessor. That is, children's lack of comprehension of an assessment task or the language of the assessment created barriers to allowing the child to reveal what he or she could do in the language (Igarashi *et al.*, 2002).

Despite these difficulties, we believed that learning as much as possible about these innovative programs was essential for the future health and credibility of foreign language education in these districts and ultimately elsewhere.

As our assessment plan evolved over time, we remained driven by the desire to explore how children learn a new language, to understand what they can achieve in the context of their respective programs and classes, and to probe the ways in which the program took root in the school curriculum or failed to do so. Our assessments always focused on describing what children can achieve in their foreign language in the elementary school (FLES) programs rather than pointing out where they exhibit gaps and deficiencies, typical of the standardized forms of assessments used in most schools. That is, we focused on what children *can do*, rather than on what they *cannot do*. In describing and explaining achievement, we included contextual factors, understanding these factors to be consequential to how children learn and what they achieve. As Hamayan (1998) has pointed out, we tried to paint a portrait of the chameleon by assessing children in the context of the classes and programs in which they learned while trying to maintain some level of comparability of findings.

Emerging questions concerning foreign language program assessment

By the end of the first three years of our research, we called this type of program evaluation the study of *ambiance* and *achievement* (see, e.g. Donato *et al.*, 1996; Chinen *et al.*, 2003; Pessoa *et al.*, 2007). These studies collectively produced a complex array of converging data points that enabled us to tell a story about the context and language development of students participating in two very different types of kindergarten through eighth grade Japanese and Spanish foreign language programs. Data reported included a statistical measure, called *growth curve analysis* (Francis *et al.*, 1991), which permitted identification of significant growth across time and changes in the level of performance of students as individuals and as members of a group. Additionally, surveys of students' attitudes concerning learning and using a foreign language and discovering a new culture, addressed, from the learners' perspective, the affective variables that influence their foreign language learning. Finally, the voices of the wider educational community (e.g. parents, grade-level teachers and foreign language teachers) were analyzed to determine their perceptions of a relatively new program within the total school curricular offerings. In this section, based on our desire for a comprehensive view of language learning in the elementary school, we present our model of program documentation, refined and modified through experience over a 15-year period.

As we began our documentation of these two innovative foreign language programs, several important issues unfolded as the programs took root in the schools. These issues derived from our goal to describe as thoroughly and comprehensively as possible the dynamics of early language learning programs and the contextual factors that contributed to program growth and student achievement. Many of the issues that we describe were shaped over time by the unique nature of the two programs. When combined, these issues and the underlying questions associated with each of them provided the framework for our research plan and provided direction for the types of information we collected and the factors we deemed important for understanding the dynamics of EFLL programs. This is not to suggest that others have not attempted to document achievement in innovative EFLL programs (Fall *et al.*, 2007) or have not examined the dynamics of early language learning (Heining-Boynton & Haitema, 2007; Cekaite, 2007). What appears unusual, however, is that early language learning has not experienced the same intense level of investigation as, for example, adult second and foreign language learning, immersion education or foreign language learning in colleges and universities.

It is ironic that early language learning has been so poorly documented and researched given that it is well known that to develop language proficiency, an individual requires extended periods of well-articulated instruction. Understanding the early stages of a learner's language learning experience is essential to understanding their history as learners, their advancement in proficiency and their performance in later years of instruction. Early language learning programs have simply not shared the same systematic and extensive research attention as other language learning contexts. This irony is perhaps best understood through the lens of the history of EFLL programs. It may well be that this lack of attention may have resulted from the ebbs and flows of these programs over time. Moreover, the lack of understanding that these programs can be rigorous and have real goals for language and culture learning may have conspired to make them less worthy of research attention. Finally, the marginalized and highly variable nature of early foreign language programs in the schools and in the minds of program constituents and researchers may have simply eclipsed any attention to the young learner.

The need for comparable data

To monitor the progress of the children, we collected information at the end of each school year concerning oral language development through interviews given to a cohort of children. Our cohort consisted of a randomly selected sample of boys and girls at specific grade levels with the goal of comparing the performance of these children as they moved through their years of study. In the case of the Japanese program, given that the program was initiated simultaneously across six grade levels (K-5), multiple assessments needed to be written. In the case of the Spanish program that used a build-up approach to implementation (see Chapter 2), ensuring that the information collected was comparable across years became paramount.

What appeared as a relatively straightforward procedure proved difficult to control when dealing with large groups of children in multiple sections of classes taught by different teachers. After the first year of each program, we realized that an end-of-year assessment could not be developed without considering the assessment tasks of the preceding year's testing. This may appear obvious to some, but in the real world of schools where a program's future has not been fully established, this vision beyond the immediate is not always readily apparent. Further, we realized that the content of the assessment needed to reflect the curriculum for each year and that we needed to craft developmentally appropriate tasks for each grade level. Without the ability to compare information across years, little could be discovered about student progress and curricular articulation. Thus, early in our assessment efforts, how to develop oral assessments that contained comparable grade level and developmentally appropriate tasks that were tied to what the students learned in their classes became an overarching question that we needed to address.

The role of the teacher

A second issue that arose concerned the role of the foreign language teacher in developing assessment tasks. The teachers in the program were essential to helping us understand the types of tasks that could be included in our oral assessments and the range of vocabulary and thematic topics that the students had learned. From this perspective, the teachers were key to providing valuable information concerning what was to be assessed and in what format. However, we soon learned that the responsibility for developing assessments to monitor student learning across time could not be delegated solely to teachers. This observation is not to disparage the good work of the teachers who were all very well aware of the content of their courses and their students' abilities. Rather, it became clear to us that teachers see their work with students from their own unique vantage point, that is, from the perspective of their own grade level, their own students and their own curriculum. Emphasizing a vision of the program beyond the confines of the individual teacher's classroom became a priority as assessments were developed collectively. It became clear that participation in assessment development and analysis had an effect on how teachers viewed the total program and their role in it.

The question that needed to be addressed, therefore, was how to include teacher participation in the assessment process while ensuring that assessments would produce valid, reliable and comparative information across years. Experience proved that the best means to achieve this goal was neither to leave teachers on their own to create assessments nor to dominate the assessment process by insisting on a particular procedure, no matter how theoretically sound or professionally sanctioned the assessment that we proposed appeared to be. We discovered over the years and through a number of initial false starts that collaborating with teachers across grade levels addressed this question directly. To develop our various assessments, teachers from various grade levels would meet with university partners and construct assessment tasks jointly, following a framework decided on by the group. That is, we designed and analyzed assessments *with* teachers rather than *for* teachers.

The cooperative assessment-designing sessions proved valuable for several reasons. First, these sessions served as a form of professional development for the teachers. They learned, for example, about issues of content validity, how to develop comparable tasks, how to draw an appropriate sample of students to be tested. By working collaboratively with the teachers, we also could be assured that the assessments we developed reflected content with which the students were familiar. Additionally, we were able to address the need for assistance during assessment, an unusual concept to most teachers who view most assessments as an independent performance with the provision of assistance understood to be cheating and illegal. To this end, we introduced concepts based on dynamic assessment (see, e.g. Lantolf & Poehner, 2007) and made principled modifications to dynamic assessment procedures for large-scale assessment where comparisons of student performance were essential and ease of reporting achievement data was a central concern.

Assessing reading and writing[1]

As the Spanish program developed and reached the middle school, other unanticipated issues emerged. Up to this point, our research efforts had been mainly on the assessment of the children's spoken proficiency. However, the content-related nature of the middle school program (grades 6–8) raised several questions concerning how students were progressing in their ability to read and write academic Spanish and their level of preparedness for the demands of a Spanish course built using academic content from four disciplines. For this reason, in 2002, we began to apply what we had learned about conducting summative oral assessments to collecting information on students' reading and writing development.

External community factors that influence learning

A question that underpinned our research from the beginning focused on the possible linkage between parental support and student achievement. Very little research had been conducted on this linkage (see Antonek et al., 1998 and Antonek, 1995, for notable exceptions); but our experience in dealing with parent groups indicated that not all parents were equally enthusiastic about the inclusion of foreign language study in the elementary and middle school. We hypothesized that positive parental attitudes might positively affect student performance. Also based on our work with parents, it became clear that they held varying beliefs about what the goals of a foreign language program should be. These beliefs often contrasted quite sharply with the explicit goals of the program and may have derived from their own personal histories as language learners. For example, if parents had negative or unproductive experiences with language learning in school when they were students, it stood to reason that they might not be able to envision foreign language education that could be otherwise. For this reason, seeking to understand the relationship between the implicit or explicit attitudes that parents conveyed in the home about foreign language learning and their children's achievement occupied an important place in our assessment plans.

Internal classroom factors that influence learning

As we analyzed end-of-year assessment information, it became apparent that classroom practice was consequential to what students were able to do in their new language. As a result, the question of instruction and its relationship to student learning and specific language performances was raised as an important issue to explore through our assessment plan. Therefore, our assessment plan included classroom observation of the teachers' instructional practices, the discursive interactions that took place between teacher and student, and the quantity and quality of student oral production during classes. We also began to explore the relationship between student and teacher oral interaction in content-based classes and student achievement on end-of-year reading and writing assessments.

This aspect of our research also showed quite dramatically the importance of formative assessments in understanding how children learned and performed in the new language. Additionally, the use of formative assessments provided us with an opportunity to know prior to summative assessments what students could do with the new language and where teachers might not have attended to important aspects of language development, such as providing adequate occasions for developing literate uses of language in academic content teaching. Formative classroom-based assessments also allowed us to track student progress in various aspects of the curriculum by analyzing student work samples that they completed with assistance rather than after instruction in independent performance at a later time.

Learner internal factors: Sustaining motivation

The extended nature of foreign language instruction presented a unique and somewhat unanticipated research opportunity to examine the students' sustained motivation as they progressed in the program. Although the question of motivation figures prominently in discussions of individual differences and second language learning (see, e.g. Dörnyei, 2001, 2005), it was not raised as a critical feature in our research until well after the students had experienced several years of language instruction. Initially, it was found in both programs that the introduction of foreign language study in the early years was enthusiastically embraced as school board members and parents took pride in the rapid accomplishments of young children. Motivation was high and program praise was abundant. However, maintaining motivation in learners and in program constituents surfaced as a concern in both programs after the initial novelty and enthusiasm for the language program dissipated. We found this aspect of early foreign language programs intriguing and a consideration that was not acknowledged directly in the literature on extended sequences of foreign language instruction. Specifically, we asked, now that we have extended sequences of instruction in place, is student motivation sufficiently strong to sustain their effort in the new language and parental interest in seeing the program continue to grow?

Programmatic Issues: Transitions and Connections

The Spanish program was unique in that there was a curricular transition from a skills-based thematic unit approach to instruction in grades K-5 to a content-related approach in the middle school (grades 6–8). Although the Spanish program used a build-up approach to implementation, that is, adding a grade level of instruction each year, fully developed curricular plans for the later years of instruction were not completed during the initial planning in the mid-1990s. Thus, when the decision to implement a content-related approach was introduced, a logical question that arose was whether the students' previous six years of instruction had adequately prepared them for the demands of using cognitive academic language (Cummins, 1979), e.g. to understand fully a science or social studies unit taught in Spanish. The ways in which students transitioned into this different instructional model became a focus of our research efforts. This transition included concerns about academic literacy development, to include reading academic texts, writing reports and participating in discussions on academic content.

Curricular issues: Content-related instruction

Also related to issues of reading and writing and transitioning from a model of instruction, which emphasized interpersonal communication, to cognitive-academic language, was the nature of instruction in courses where Spanish became the vehicle for learning Spanish while simultaneously supporting and learning academic subject-matter content. We also wanted to understand how teachers carried out content-based instruction (CBI) given that this approach rarely receives extensive and thorough attention in teacher preparation programs or in methodology textbooks.

Learning a 'second foreign language'

In the Spanish program, we also had a unique opportunity to examine closely the addition of a second foreign language in the curriculum. In this program, when students entered grade 8, they were given elective course options of studying German or French. Based on several observational reports from German and French teachers on the positive performance of these second foreign language learners, we examined the effects that learning a foreign language in grades K-7 might have on students who opted to study a second foreign language during grade 8 and in high school. Thus, the question to emerge was what differences might appear in how experienced foreign language learners learn a second foreign language in the upper grades. Questions focused on the types of learning strategies the students used, the ease of acquisition of new vocabulary, their tolerance for ambiguity and target language use in the classroom, and their sophistication in understanding the grammar and morphology of the second foreign language.

Language retention and loss

In contrast to the Spanish program, the Japanese program was discontinued in 2005 when, quite unexpectedly, the single itinerant Japanese language teacher resigned a month before the opening of school. We were in a unique position, therefore, to ask a fundamental question concerning language attrition. What do students retain of the language that they had studied for several years, a year after instruction had ceased? This question involved examining students' retention of the most basic formulaic expressions, their ability to use language creatively and their retention of cultural information in the form of stories and cultural practices.

Students with learning disabilities

The Spanish program, located in a large public school district, faced many questions concerning the teaching of foreign language to students with identified learning disabilities. A number of parents and teachers expressed concern that the time taken away from first language reading and mathematics for Spanish study would interfere with a child's first language development and achievement in other high-stakes testing subjects. School administrators who dealt with the Spanish program were not particularly well prepared to address these issues with parents and found little empirical research to support the school district's practice of a full-inclusion Spanish program. For this reason, understanding how students with identified learning disabilities fared in foreign language classes, what they could achieve, what instructional accommodations assisted their learning and what positive consequences resulted from their foreign language study became central questions. Additionally, we knew that the scant research that existed on this topic was conducted on beginning language learners. It was a widespread and commonly held belief that during the initial stages of language learning where the 'playing field' was level for all students, students with disabilities were at par and sometimes outperformed regular education students. What surfaced as a key issue, given the extended programs in which we worked, was how students with disabilities fared over time and whether variability in achievement or learning problems would surface beyond the basics and after several years of instruction. In this regard, we began to disaggregate data based on students who were identified as having learning disabilities in both programs. In the Japanese program, we examined differences in Kanji writing between students with learning disabilities and other students. In the Spanish program and at the time of this writing, a doctoral student and member of the research team is completing her dissertation research on a close analysis of two students with learning disabilities in grade 6 Spanish who have been with the Spanish program since its inception.

Language development over time

A central question throughout all of our research focused on language development, that is, how do children learn a second language and how does this ability grow and change over time. We looked at spoken and written language development from several different perspectives. We were interested in various aspects of a child's language development, including the development of pronunciation, morphology (e.g. particles in Japanese and verb morphology in Spanish), syntactic diversity, vocabulary, discourse and the ability to carry out a range of language functions in speech and writing. We were also interested in differences in the growth of these language features both for groups of students (e.g. members of the so-called cohort whom we had been following since program inception versus newcomers, low achievers versus high achievers, native speakers versus non-native speakers) and within individual students at the same grade level and in the same class (see the use of growth curve analysis in Donato et al., 1996). Perhaps more than any other question, this concern for individual differences was central to any information gathering that we conducted.

We also attempted to understand how the second language ability of a student who performed at the novice level could be better described given that what was available were merely global and general descriptions based on adult performance. Moreover, our work with assessing language development in children led us to realize that these adult descriptions that had been adopted did not satisfactorily differentiate well the trajectory of language development among children and did not capture the complexity of novice-level language development. What was available often described this level of performance by referring to only the most rudimentary language operations, such as the use of memorized phases, listing vocabulary and reactive language production. This concern led us to ask whether early language learners are categorically novices defined in our limited ways of understanding novice performance. Stated differently, the question to be answered was 'what does a novice actually look like' in the elementary school (Igarashi et al., 2002).

Principles of Assessment

Five overarching principles or goals guided our research as we answered the 12 essential questions discussed above. First, in all aspects of the research, we sought to understand what children *could do* with their new language, no matter how limited their language resources might be, rather than what they could not do. Much of the work on language assessment is based on identifying deficiencies and gaps in knowledge rather than exploring how learners make use of their knowledge resources, including the assistance of others. Within the context of describing the positive aspects of a child's performance, we were also able to examine empirically what the profession held to be acceptable levels of performance through an examination of professionally agreed-on documents, such as the Student Oral Proficiency Assessment (Center for Applied Linguistics, 2007). To provide assessments that highlighted what children could do required constant communication with teachers about their lessons, observations of classroom instruction, formative assessments for insight into the children's developing language competence, and knowledge of student attitudes and other constituents that may explain performance.

A second guiding principle involved our undertaking a *multiple perspectives analysis* of student achievement and program ambiance. We believe that no single measure can accurately and robustly capture the myriad factors that we observed when describing, analyzing and interpreting the successes and challenges of the two programs in which we worked. For this reason, the story that we tell consists of a multiple array of data points that converge, complement and, at times, diverge and lead to more questions and implications for early language learning programs. As we progressed in our research, it became clear that linkages existed between, for example, student attitude and achievement and teacher-student interactions and the development of spoken interactional competence. These linkages allowed us to explain what we observed rather than just providing surface level descriptions or uninformed observations of the dynamics of the program.

A third principle that we focused on was *change over time*. Few, if any, longitudinal studies of language development and program implementation exist despite repeated recommendations in the literature for carrying out such studies (Tucker, 1999; Collier, 1991; Collier & Thomas, 2004). Describing and analyzing the life of the program required comparisons of various aspects of the program year-to-year. The achievement of the students needed to be compared as they progressed in their programs and the attitudes of students, teachers and parents needed to be monitored after the novelty and excitement of the new programs waned.

By far, conducting a rigorous longitudinal assessment was the most challenging aspect of this research because of an understandable inability to anticipate the emergence of new and vexing issues, changes in demographics or modifications in school policies for scheduling foreign language instruction. For example, as confidence in the Japanese program began to waiver and time for instruction became scarce, scheduling anomalies emerged and reductions in instructional time took place. Despite these difficulties, we remained vigilant to the importance of establishing useable linkages in the data. We succeeded in collecting multiple sources of data from various perspectives that allowed us to describe the genesis of the two programs, their growth and the obstacles to their expansion, and, in the case of one program, the ultimate elimination of the program from the school's curricular offerings.

A fourth goal, related to the collection and analysis of comparative data over time, involved *comparisons among students who participated in the program for various lengths of time*. Therefore, we identified a group that we referred to as *cohort students* – those who began the language program in kindergarten and remained in it throughout their school careers. Since we wished to be able to monitor, describe and analyze the outcomes of a well-articulated sequence of K-8 instruction, given the dearth of programs of this type in the USA and the lack of available data on this particular type of instruction, the identification of cohort students became the group against which we compared and contrasted the performance of other students. We attempted to understand how children who participated in the program from the start performed relative to those students who entered the program at various start-times after the kindergarten year. Referred to as *newcomers*, these children became focal points for comparison with the cohort students against whom we examined differential aspects of language leaning, such as the development of written syntax, oral language development and attitude comparisons.

A further use of the cohort permitted close examination of target students on a range of learning experiences. Described as profiles of success, we attempted to depict, through comparisons of target students within the cohort, what contributed to language learning, or prevented it. We also made use of individual target students for comparing the performance of selected newcomers to selected children in the cohort. By closely examining target students and moving beyond aggregated data, we were able to capture a range of factors that might have been hidden from view if we had not taken into consideration the uniqueness of individuals and what they bring as individuals to the task of learning a new language.

A final overarching principle concerned *how we could communicate the results of this research effectively to multiple audiences* and how we could make the research accessible to non-specialists in the field. Many of the non-specialist consumers of our research were major stakeholders and decision makers whose opinions often affected the future of the program. For example, school board members and parents needed to understand the program in ways that went beyond their own preconceived views of what could be achieved in a foreign language classroom. Often the recipients themselves of negative or unsuccessful foreign language learning experiences, parents and school board members needed to understand clearly how the program was being implemented, how children were progressing and what were realistic performance expectations. Moreover, the teachers themselves needed to understand the results of end-of-year testing and how these results might influence their curricula and lead to change from year to year. For these reasons, we investigated ways to report the results of our research in various forms, such as teacher-led research reports to other teachers, user-friendly summaries, visual and graphic displays, oral presentations as well as traditional research publications in professional journals. As time progressed, we also discovered that involving teachers directly in the research, as researchers and interpreters of research, was among the best ways to educate and make accessible the ways in which research contributes to understanding and improving their programs. As collaborators on the research, their involvement involved small-scale action research (Donato, 2002, 2003) leading the teachers to experience what it is to be a fully contributing member of a research team.

Areas of Assessment

The guiding principles for selecting areas and methods for assessment were threefold. First, we wanted to ensure that we collected data that were informative and useful to teachers, administrators and parents. Second, we wanted to be able, when circumstances permitted, to identify cohorts of students whom we could follow over time since there is such a paucity of longitudinal data to inform language education planning and program implementation. Finally, we wanted to use, when possible, measures that were not idiosyncratic, but were well known and widely used by members of the language profession. We now provide a general description of the measures that we used to assess and to document student growth and development in the two programs.

Oral proficiency

In the initial years of our work at early grade levels, we wished to focus on the students' development of oral proficiency so we adapted a form of the American Council on Teaching of Foreign Languages (ACTFL) Oral Proficiency Interview (OPI), which has been developed and refined by members of the US government's Interagency Language Roundtable (ILR). The ILR includes representatives from various federal agencies that have a need for individuals with a high degree of foreign language proficiency in their positions. The ACTFL adapted these descriptors, initially developed for adults working in language-sensitive positions, for use with university students (see Shrum & Glisan, 2009, for a history of the development of the ACTFL proficiency scales for speaking). Later, the procedure and the scoring template was further adapted, under the leadership of the Center for Applied Linguistics, for use with school-age youngsters.

We conducted standard interviews with students, using a variety of prompts intended to check comprehension and to elicit production about familiar topics introduced during the school year (e.g. in the early grades, a focus on classroom objects, food, weather, clothes, greetings, family members). The assessment we used can best be characterized as a prochievement interview (PRO-I) or one that attempts to combine a measure of the child's proficiency as filtered through the achievement that can realistically be expected by someone at a particular age and grade level (for more detailed information, see Donato et al., 1994). This interview allowed us to assess student performance in a meaningful and realistic context on lexical, grammatical and discursive items presented in class and included in a particular curriculum. Interviewers were native speakers, or advanced level speakers of Japanese or Spanish who were familiarized with OPI guidelines, conducted mock interviews and used a Student Observation Form (SOF; adapted from the Student Oral Language Observation Matrix, San Jose, n.d.), which called for ratings on five scales – comprehension, fluency, vocabulary, pronunciation and grammar. At the conclusion of the interview, an observer assigned a PRO-I rating to each of the children using the ACTFL oral proficiency rating scale for Japanese or for Spanish.

As we refined our oral assessments, we realized that eliciting speech from children was difficult given their limited range of vocabulary and structures and the children's emotional reactions (e.g. shyness, anxiety, fear) to a face-to-face interview in a language other than their own. For this reason, we explored ways to elicit speech from children that was appropriate for their age and that was non-threatening. We discovered that children were quite willing to talk about topics with which they were familiar and which were close to their lived experiences. Oller (1998) refers to these forms of orally produced texts as true narrative representations (TNR) and claims that as discourse comes to more closely resemble TNR, it becomes more comprehensible and thus more learnable, to which we would add that it can be more clearly assessed. In the Spanish program as a way of ensuring TNRs for assessing language development, we used drawings that the children produced themselves in their classes that represented themes and topics introduced in their Spanish classes as the basis for eliciting speech samples. In this way, what the children produced and narrated were true representations of how they experienced their learning rather than a researcher's view of what children should know and do. By using this approach, we found that children were quite willing and excited to explain their drawings to us during this portion of the oral assessment and that the quantity of production increased significantly compared with standard question-answer interview formats.

We also learned that assistance must be provided dynamically during oral assessments to capture the range of abilities of what children knew and could do (Lantolf & Poehner, 2007). Prompts during the assessment tasks ranged from implicit and minimal cues to explicit and overt assistance. In this way, we were able to better differentiate various levels of performance beyond what the response to the solitary question could yield. The use of assistance during interviews also provided a non-threatening testing environment for the children. Given the large number of students, we also found that predetermining the types of assistance that interviewers provided was an effective way to make comparisons across individual students. Although not entirely consistent with the orthodox theory of dynamic assessment, our modified interventionist approach worked well in the context of testing large numbers of students (see Lantolf & Poehner, 2007, for a thorough discussion of the two traditions in dynamic assessment and their relationship to development).

Closely associated with the issues involved in dynamic assessment was the type of assistance provided. We learned throughout the years of administering oral assessments to children, that at times, they would not respond to prompts in the target language, but that they responded in Spanish or Japanese quite well when the interviewer questioned them or made comments in English (the first language of all these children). What we realized was that it was unrealistic to expect children (and perhaps adults, as well) to demonstrate interactional competence entirely in the new language. Rather, learners often exhibited a mix of first and foreign languages while interacting with the interviewers. Additionally, the use of English appeared to remove obstacles to comprehension that inhibited the children's use of the target language.

Finally, in an effort to capture what students knew rather than where they were deficient, oral assessments needed to reflect closely the types of topics, tasks and talk with which students had experience in the classroom. One way this issue was addressed was to administer vocabulary screening tests before constructing the oral assessment protocol. By establishing a certain criterion level of performance on baseline vocabulary items, we were assured that our assessment tasks would be comprehensible to the children and performance would not be hindered by lack of vocabulary knowledge.[2]

It is worth noting that on various occasions we also used variations of the 'imitation, comprehension and production' data-collection format developed and popularized by Fraser *et al.* (1963), in which students were asked to repeat utterances in the target language that were successively longer and longer, thus exceeding the students' short-term memory capacity. This elicited repetition procedure also required the children to attend to meaning and syntax to complete the task since memory capacity for mere repetition was exceeded. As Lantolf (2003) has argued, the fundamental difference between repetition and imitation is that imitation demands understanding the meaning of what learners select to say within their respective zones of proximal development. By contrast, repetition and reproduction is limited because of an individual' inability to grasp the meaningfulness and structure of an action. We also mapped the children's ability to repeat and imitate progressively longer utterances onto the children's oral language production in the classroom, to explore the consequences of classroom discursive practices and the children's ability to imitate the interviewer' sentences.

Related to assessing the interactive communicative ability of the children, we realized that we needed to understand how they participated in interactions that permitted them to observe interactional moves, reflect on them and create their own active construction of responses to these patterns (Hall, 1995). These data complemented our end-of-year assessment data and helped us better understand why students performed in particular ways. For example, in the middle school grades, we focused on the ways in which students and teachers were using oral language in the classroom in the service of their CBI (i.e. the integration of Spanish and social studies, Spanish and science, etc.). To collect data on the discourse of CBI, informal observations were conducted throughout a school year of two sixth grade foreign language classrooms. Over the course of the year, four class periods of each teacher were videotaped and transcribed. Raters worked inductively from the data and selected the discursive features that were recurrent and emerged from the instructional tasks that were used by each teacher. The features of the teachers' talk revealed how these two teachers explored and discussed academic content discursively with their students and, thus, supported their development of interactive competence and academic content knowledge. Thus, in these data, we attempted to isolate discourse features that enabled discussions about academic content while simultaneously supporting the development of foreign language proficiency, an overarching goal of all CBI programs. The discourse features that we examined were (a) language-related talk and content-related talk, (b) conversation features of interpersonal communication, (c) the use of English and (d) teacher feedback and error correction (see Pessoa *et al.*, 2007, for a fuller description of the methodology).

Vocabulary development

In our early work with students in the Japanese program, we focused on assessing vocabulary *per se*, taking vocabulary development as a kind of additional 'proxy' for language growth or development. For this purpose, adaptations of the widely used Peabody Picture Vocabulary Test (2006) were administered. Although this measure was useful, we did not continue to do isolated vocabulary assessment in later years; rather vocabulary development was assessed within the context of reading and writing assessments.

Academic literacy development: Reading and writing in content-based instruction

As the students progressed to the middle school (grades 6–8), we began to assess their literacy development. This included an assessment of their reading *and* writing skills using authentic, performance-based tasks that were developed in collaboration with the participating teachers to reflect the literacy demands that were made on the students in their classes. For example, on one occasion the task directed students to write a letter to the Environmental Protection Agency discussing and comparing various natural resources in the community, while on another, students were prompted to write a letter to a friend who lives in a Spanish-speaking country and who is planning a trip to the child's hometown. In these cases, each student's writing was evaluated by two raters using a modified version of the ACTFL rubric for presentational mode of communication (see Glisan *et al.*, 2003 for rubrics) for intermediate learners. Student writing was scored on the following categories: language function, text type, impact, vocabulary, comprehensibility and language control. Each of the six components was assigned a score ranging from zero to three. Two raters evaluated the 12 writing samples individually, compared scores and established inter-rater agreement on the scores for the 12 assessments.

For the *language function* criterion, each student's writing was assessed in terms of their ability to describe, compare, elaborate and begin to use connectors such as 'porque' [because] and 'pero' [but]. In looking at *text type* and *impact*, the writing was assessed for quantity of sentences, organization of the language, examples of varied sentence structure and attention to audience. For *vocabulary*, raters assessed students' appropriate use of the lexical items provided and their attempt to include additional related vocabulary and phrases. With reference to *comprehensibility*, student writing was examined for the ease with which it could be understood by an individual unaccustomed to the writing of language learners. Finally, *language control* was assessed by looking at the accuracy of descriptions, comparisons, negative sentences, gender and number agreement and use of verb conjugations (for a more detailed description, see Pessoa *et al.*, 2007).

Although seemingly comprehensive in its features, the ACTFL rubrics failed to capture some important linguistic and functional aspects of the children's literacy development. That is, lurking in the margins of all these aspects of writing for which detailed criteria have been developed, we noted differences that went beyond appropriate functional and structural production of the text and global comprehensibility by an audience of readers. We turned to the work of Halliday (1975) and began to code texts for functional categories as specified in his systemic functional linguistics (SFL) theory. These functional categories are not genre-specific and represent a level of analysis between typical functions (e.g. describing) and the use of morphosyntax. That is, Halliday's categories (e.g. heuristic, personal, regulatory, etc.) can be used in a variety of text types to realize an individual writer's intentions. A descriptive essay could, for example, provide personal opinions, direct the reader to attend to some aspect of the description or provide an explanation. A particular genre is rarely monolithic, often mixing freely with other genres during text production (e.g. a narrative might provide description or instruct or be woven with the personal opinion of the author). The SFL framework provided the close analysis of text that we needed to document progress and describe differences in various types of students and on various tasks.

Student questionnaires

At various grades, we assessed the attitudes and motivation of the participating students. Based on the work of Gardner (1985), we adapted sets of questionnaires to be age and grade-level appropriate. In these questionnaires, typically completed by students in their language class, we asked about topics such as their level of engagement and of enjoyment, their use of language outside the classroom, the likelihood that they would continue their study of the language and perceptions of their parents' support for their language study, among other issues (see, e.g. Donato *et al.*, 2000).

We also collected information about the students' perceptions of their own developing second language abilities. For this purpose, we adapted grade-appropriate versions of the so-called 'Can Do' questionnaires developed by Clark (1981) at the Educational Testing Service. The advantage of this type of questionnaire as opposed to the typical self-assessment is that the Can Do questionnaire asks the student to think about what they *can do* in a context-specific situation with respect to speaking, reading, listening or writing, depending on the grade level. Additionally, the Can Do questionnaire asked students to rate their ability while thinking about a peer of the same age rather than in relation to their teachers. For example, a student might be asked to indicate with what degree of ease (on a three- or five-point scale) they would be able to 'say the days of the week', 'give directions to the local police station to someone' and 'discuss the pros and cons of an editorial that appeared in the local newspaper', relative to a peer in the class. We also took this opportunity to ask students about areas of ability where they assessed themselves as needing more work. Not surprisingly, there was a strong correlation between what children claimed they could not do with their own personal learning goals.

Teacher questionnaires

On various occasions, we took the opportunity to gather information systematically about teacher attitudes, knowledge and beliefs about the program from both the language teachers as well as from other teachers in the schools. We asked questions about topics such as their awareness of the program, opinions about the program, what type of feedback, if any, they received from parents, and about the collaboration (or lack thereof) among the language teachers and the other grade level teachers. Gaining access to the foreign language teachers thinking also took the form of narrative written reflections at the end of each year, and observations of teacher comments during group meetings and planning sessions.

Parent questionnaires

We also periodically collected information from parents about their views toward the programs, their expectations concerning the foci of instruction as well as what they would consider to be the most important outcomes of the programs. Typically, paper-and-pencil questionnaires were developed and mailed home to parents with the request that they complete them and return them to one of the authors. Parental questionnaires asked for demographic information, language-learning history, personal opinions about the value of foreign language study and attitudes toward the goals of a foreign language program. Anonymity was assured, although the parents were also provided with an opportunity for personal telephone or electronic follow-up should they wish to do so.

Parent tracer study

We also had the opportunity to do a type of *tracer* study to collect information from the parents of the 'graduates' of the Japanese program – that is, from the parents of students who had completed grade 8 of the Japanese program and made the transition to other schools in the area. We constructed a parent questionnaire that asked for information about whether Japanese was available in the schools that the students were now attending, and if so, whether they were continuing their study; what the parents thought in retrospect about the program and whether they believed that it made a good contribution to the overall educational experience of their child.

The influence of assessment on classroom instruction: Curricular innovations

As work continued, particularly within the Spanish program, and the students progressed toward the middle school where Spanish would be taught for 40 minutes per day through a content-based or content-related approach, we knew that it would be important for the students to have a level of literacy skills to permit them to read and discuss challenging texts and learn academic content from them. The results of end-of-year assessments in the intermediate grades 3–5 raised cause for concern so we initiated a program of teacher-action research, coordinated by then-doctoral student Rocío Domínguez, in which teachers were encouraged, and guided, to infuse literacy across their curricula.

Concerns raised by the Spanish teachers in grades K-4 and by the principal of the intermediate school about Spanish literacy development in grades 3-4 motivated developing a procedure for working collaboratively with the Spanish teachers over the course of the 2001–2002 school year. This procedure led to curricular discussion, innovation and reform. During that school year, the Spanish teachers were expected to discuss and determine goals for Spanish literacy in grades K-5 and to implement these goals, as well. At the first meeting, Olivia, a new faculty member, suggested using an innovative foreign language method called PACE (Presentation, Attention, Co-construction and Extension) for implementing Spanish literacy in grades K-5, which she reported using for her lessons.

The PACE model embraces a content-based approach to foreign language instruction. It was developed by Donato (see Adair-Hauck et al., 1994) for implementing standards-based foreign language instruction that integrated meaningful content and focus on form. PACE is grounded in both Vygotskyan psycholinguistics and uses a story-telling approach. Aside from discussing and determining Spanish literacy goals, the Spanish teachers were expected to implement PACE one time during the year. A unit lesson can span three to four weeks for a daily 20-minute class in grades K-5; thus, the implementation of a PACE lesson for one unit lesson was expected to be time consuming for teachers in that they needed to design new activities and prepare new materials. Finally, we presumed that some parts of the PACE model might be perceived as challenging for teachers. According to the Spanish teachers, they were unaccustomed to introducing stories to their students, and thus, we expect that PACE would be perceived as very different in that respect, since this method advocates presenting language in meaningful cultural texts before turning attention to the formal properties of the text that render it meaningful. From this perspective, the PACE model differed significantly from the traditional paradigm of vocabulary and grammar practice before meaningful language use.

Data came from multiple sources such as documents, various perspectives on the innovation by the teachers and classroom observation. By combining multiple sources, our aim was to add rigor to the research. In line with Denzin and Lincoln (2002: 5), 'the use of multiple methods, or triangulation, [in qualitative research] reflects an attempt to secure an in-depth understanding of the phenomenon in question'. Our data came from eight sources: (1) the transcriptions and notes of regular monthly meetings with the Spanish teachers, (2) copies of a teacher's notes of the meetings, (3) teachers' questionnaire and check-list, (4) transcriptions and notes of individual interviews with the K-5 Spanish teachers and administrators, (5) transcriptions and notes of classroom observations in grades 3–4, (6) copies of teachers' relevant lesson plans (2000–2001; 2001–2002) in grades 3–4, (7) teachers' student reports and (8) K-5 Spanish curricula (September, 2001; June, 2002).

Data gathered were examined in order to find evidence of changes in the curricula. These pieces of data were, in turn, compared to teachers' lesson plans (2001–2002) and to portions of the Spanish curricula in grades 3–4 for evidence of change. As a member check, a copy of the data analysis was given to all the Spanish teachers, for their review and comment. This practice allowed the researcher to address ethical concerns and ensure discretion by letting each teacher corroborate *her own* interpretation of the data. The purpose was to avoid missing points and possible misunderstandings, and to add triangulation to the data analysis.

Cohort versus non-cohort

Another important aspect of our research with both groups of students in the Japanese program and in the Spanish program was to track students over time to look at their cumulative progress. Our general approach to this was the same in both programs. From the kindergarten group, we selected two boys and two girls in each of the classrooms in which the language was offered and we followed these students 'cohort students' over time, usually collecting information (e.g. oral proficiency assessment, reading and writing assessments, etc.) during the latter part of the school year. Although we regularly collected a variety of data from other students, we tried to ensure that we regularly, and systematically, collected information from the so-called cohort students so that we would be able to track their progress longitudinally and also so that we would be able to make other comparisons that might interest administrators and other foreign language professionals.

Cohort versus newcomer

For example, in some of our comparisons, we look specifically at the way in which a newcomer to the program performs on a variety of oral, reading and writing tasks in relationship to others who have been in the foreign language program since kindergarten. This has been an important topic of continuing conversation because the Spanish school has established a number of programs for newcomers to the district. For example, a short intensive summer experience, known as the *Amigos* program, paired a newcomer with a student in the same grade who had been in the program since kindergarten. The Japanese school made no particular provision for newcomers.

Early versus late start (K-2 versus 3-5)

We also looked carefully in some of our assessments at the relative performance of students who began the Spanish program in kindergarten versus groups of students who transferred into the school district and began the study of Spanish at grade 3 or grade 6 and thus did not have the opportunity for an early start. There is much debate in the literature about whether there are advantages that accrue to students who have the opportunity for an early start; but there are remarkably few data. We believe that our work sheds light on this continually vexing question.

Summary

In this chapter, we have outlined our model of assessment used in these two programs. We have shown through this model the myriad factors that come into play when trying to describe EFLL programs and to analyze how children acquire competence in a foreign language. Taken collectively, these factors reveal the complexity of early language learning programs. Several critical and unresolved issues have been raised that could potentially have a negative effect on a program's ability to sustain itself after initial enthusiasm and support subside. For example, student motivation over time, positive parental attitudes toward language learning in the home, and a consistent and coherent vision of a sequential program are only a few of the factors that need to be in place to sustain foreign language programs that seem to be viewed in the history of education as endemically non-essential and marginal.

In the next chapter, we review some of the findings on these issues from selected studies that we have conducted over the past 16 years. It is our hope that these findings will create, at least in part, a research base for early language programs; will identify areas that require further investigation; and will provide a better understanding of why some foreign language programs thrive while others wither away and fold.

Notes

1. We refer to this aspect of our assessments as reading and writing. We opt for this terminology to reflect what became an essential question driving the research. Are children progressing in their ability to read texts for meaning and write with a purpose and addressed to a particular audience? Although all assessment tasks involved presentation to an audience and interpreting texts beyond factual recall, early assessment tasks were clearly divided between reading and writing, with later tasks integrating the reading passage with the writing task. Given the broad and encompassing nature of the terms presentational and interpretive modes of communication, we think it best to reflect clearly our assessment goals and procedures and avoid professional jargon that may lead to confusion.
2. This general approach is also described in Donato *et al.* (1994, 1996) and in Tucker *et al.* (1996). We also wish to call the readers' attention to the very helpful online Foreign Language Assessment Directory (FLAD) developed and maintained by staff at the Center for Applied Linguistics in Washington, DC (http://www.cal.org/CALWebDB/FLAD/). This directory can be searched free of charge, and users are asked to contribute their own assessment instruments for possible inclusion.

Chapter 4
Documenting Student Language Achievement

The purpose of this chapter is to present findings from the research that we described in Chapter 3. The research reported in this chapter covers both oral and written language development and presents findings that describe what children can do in sequential early foreign language programs. We believe that this research offers clear support for providing students with an early start to foreign language instruction. The research findings also begin to give shape to a research base on early language learning and delineate fruitful areas for further inquiry.

As the following overview will show, an important aspect of this research was to document as thoroughly as possible the achievements of students in the program at various grade levels and as *groups* (e.g. cohort versus non-cohort, early starters versus newcomers, grade level differences) and *individuals* with unique abilities, attitudes and achievement. Our assessments, as described in Chapter 3, included documenting proficiency in speaking and writing, examining student self-assessments of their own developing abilities, and monitoring their growth in cultural knowledge and willingness to communicate with speakers of Japanese and Spanish outside class. We also examined individual students more closely to develop profiles of particular types of learners to include both successful students as well as those who appeared to struggle with language learning or exhibited disengagement in the process. These individual profiles provided depth to our data and added significantly to our understanding of how children learn in elementary and middle school programs.

In this section, we will review several studies from our previous research that document students' cumulative oral and written language development and relationships, if any, between classroom instruction and performance on oral and writing tasks. Our work in the Japanese program focused primarily on oral language development. Studies of the development of foreign language written proficiency were carried out predominantly in the Spanish program. One reason for this separation of skill by school is that mastery of written language was not a priority for the Japanese program aside from having the students learn a few formulaic words, such as their name, days of the week, etc., which were presented in the context of theme-based lessons. By contrast, the focus on content-based instruction in the Spanish program promoted attention to literacy issues, namely, reading academic texts and producing expository writing. For this reason, end-of-year assessments closely examined the Spanish students' progress in these domains of language use. We have also organized the research longitudinally to allow for yearly comparisons and to show how longitudinal assessment goes beyond single test administrations in capturing students' emerging language abilities.

Students' Cumulative Oral Language Development: Year 1 of JFL

Our first investigation of students' oral language development took place in spring 1993, the end of the first year of the Japanese program (for a complete description of the year 1 Japanese as a foreign language (JFL) study, see Donato et al., 1994). We selected a stratified random sample of 32 target students – two boys and two girls from each of the eight classes that comprised the K-5 program at the time. Each student was interviewed using a standard interview procedure that required students to produce samples of speech on familiar topics based on the curriculum (greetings, classroom objects, clothing, weather, etc.). We described our testing procedures as a prochievement interview (Pro-I) since we assessed students' spoken language ability in realistic communicative contexts using language material with which they were familiar. Each interview lasted 10–12 minutes – a length that we determined was reasonable for children at this age. As one research assistant conducted the interview of each student, a second observed the interview and assigned a rating using a Student Observation Form (SOF) that we adapted from the Student Oral Language Observation Matrix (San Jose, n.d.). The SOF contained descriptors for five features of oral performance – comprehension, fluency, vocabulary, pronunciation and grammar. The second assistant (the observer) also assigned a global Pro-I rating based on the American Council on the Teaching of Foreign Languages (ACTFL) scales, thereby allowing the first assistant to focus on the interview task itself.

The results of year 1 testing provided an exciting profile of the development of oral language proficiency particularly when one considers that all the children were true beginners and that they had only 15 minutes of Japanese instruction per day, resulting in 45 hours of total language instruction for the academic year. Fourteen children received scores in the novice-mid to novice-high range and 18 children received scores in the novice-low category. Our ratings were based on the criteria established in the ACTFL proficiency guidelines for novice speakers (ACTFL, 1999). The rating of novice ability implies that all students were, in fact, able to perform orally in Japanese and that all children were able to participate in some, if not all, of the interview tasks. This demonstrated performance along the continuum of novice ability indicated that these children were 'on the chart' and beginning to develop proficiency in Japanese.

In addition to assigning the composite Pro-I score, the observer also rated each of the students across five language features on a five-point scale (1 = lowest and 5 = highest) using the SOF (see above). An examination of the means of the observer's score for each section of the SOF indicated that the students performed best in pronunciation followed by vocabulary, comprehension, fluency and grammar. We also asked the teacher to rate each of the 32 students using the SOF and found significant correlations between the teacher's ratings and the observer's ratings for all categories except pronunciation ($r = -0.19$). A t-test also revealed a significant difference in the rating by the observer and the teacher on the feature of fluency. For fluency, the teacher rated students consistently lower ($x = 2.08$) than the observer ($x = 2.45$; $t = 2.63$, $p < 0.001$). This finding was not surprising given the curricular emphasis on strong comprehension skills and the teacher's expectations of what children should be able to comprehend. Conversely, when asked to assess production, the teacher had very little practice in assessing speaking and little, if any, prior knowledge of student performance for making comparisons and judgments. We concluded our analysis by correlating the teacher's and the observer's SOF score and the Pro-I global rating, and found a significant correlation between these two measures ($r = 0.69$). Thus, we concluded that our measures were reliable and this increased our confidence in the teacher's ability to assess students accurately, a theme that we have documented across several of our published studies.

We ended year 1 of our association with the Japanese program on an optimistic note. We noted that the children appeared to be making steady progress in their oral language development despite the relatively brief instructional time allocated to foreign language learning relative to other subject areas and the marginalized status of foreign language study in the school's total curriculum. The results from year 1 clearly indicated that a foreign language in the elementary school program of this type had the potential for developing much greater language ability in young children than might be expected from the foreign language exploratory (FLEX) models of language study that were so popular during this time.

Students' Cumulative Oral Language Development: Year 3 of JFL

During the third year of the JFL program (1995–1996), we continued to explore the language gains made by the children. Despite a change of teacher and lukewarm enthusiasm toward the program on the part of colleagues, the program appeared to be moving forward and taking hold in the school. The new teacher introduced modifications to the curriculum that included cultural storytelling activities and opportunities for students to retell and create their own stories, thus providing occasions for language production, an area that had been missing in previous years.[1]

In addition to our end-of-year oral language assessment in year 3, we also included a vocabulary measure that we administered three times (October 1994, January 1995, May 1995). The vocabulary measure was adapted from the Peabody Picture Vocabulary Test and contained 25 individually administered oral items. On each, the child listened and selected one picture, from among four choices, that represented the item named by the research assistant. The purpose for administering the test three times was to capture growth over time using a statistical procedure called growth curve analysis (GCA) (see below).

We have previously described the oral interviews (see Donato et al., 1994) as Pro-I because tasks were linked to the curriculum and were proficiency oriented.[2] Each of the target students was interviewed by a native speaker of Japanese who used a standard pre-tested protocol with a variety of tasks that were used to elicit samples of Japanese. The format of the Pro-I included: (1) warm-up (e.g. general greetings, name, etc.), (2) focused and open-ended questions about a picture of a familiar household scene, (3) a set of grammaticality judgments in which the child had to choose which of two alternatives sounded 'better', (4) several forced-choice questions, (5) a set of elicited repetition items presented in Japanese (e.g. apple, red apple, red apple on the table, red apple on the brown table, the red apple is on the brown table in the living room) and (6) a wrap-up session in which the child was asked to name as many of the objects as possible from a picture and to count from one to ten. Interview sessions were video-recorded and lasted from 12 to 15 minutes. Similar to year 1 of the study, a second observer, a native-speaker of Japanese, assessed the child's performance using a SOF. The observer assessed the children's oral ability along a five-point scale on a set of five dimensions of language use – comprehension, fluency, vocabulary, pronunciation and grammar. At the conclusion of the Pro-I, the observer, guided by the ACTFL oral proficiency rating scale, also assigned a 'global' rating (e.g. novice-low, intermediate-mid, etc.) to each of the children. Each of these ratings (the individual dimensions of the SOF and the global Pro-I) contributed to the GCA discussed below.

A GCA was conducted using a sample of 28 children for whom we had data across four testing events (May, 1994, September, 1994, January 1995, May 1995). The data from these selected 28 children, who were representative of the school's population based on similar performances in reading and language arts on the California Achievement Test, were used for documenting and charting language development over time.

A GCA is a statistical measure differing from the traditional models of trend analysis. A GCA attempts to capture growth and change for each individual separately and for groups of individuals collectively (Francis *et al.*, 1991: 616). A major difference between the GCA and trend analysis is that the latter allows growth parameters to vary, but *only* across groups of subjects; within-group, individual variability in growth parameters is considered an error. By contrast, the GCA posits a different unit of quantifiable analysis, the individual, and formulates a model of change focusing the study of development on interindividual differences in intraindividual change. Further, as Francis *et al.* (1991: 609–610) point out, a compelling alternative to traditional formulation of change is to consider change as reflecting a continuous process that underlies performance. That is, in developmental contexts, quantitative change is more naturally represented as ongoing and continuous growth within individuals. Thus, *individuals* within research samples can display unique underlying growth trajectories and, therefore, this type of analysis can elucidate the *process* of change within a sample, not simply the amount of change taking place in the sample as a whole at arbitrary points in time during the unfolding of this process.

Individual differences in oral language development: Growth curve analysis

The Pro-I yielded six distinct measures of competence in Japanese (total Pro-I score, vocabulary, grammatical control, pronunciation, comprehension and fluency) and the Japanese Picture Vocabulary Test

(JPVT) added an additional vocabulary measure to the profile of each student in the sample. Therefore, the CGA permitted us to view significant growth, stability or backsliding across these seven measures. Additionally, since the GCA captured development in discrete components of JFL ability for each individual, a better understanding of the nature of change in the linguistic growth of individuals from year 2 to year 3 on the Pro-I could be achieved. The following results of the GCA represent, therefore, an account of how these individual students grew in a JFL program in different ways, their areas of achievement and the dimensions of growth that in the past may have remained hidden if one looked exclusively at aggregate scores or global proficiency ratings.

The GCA revealed that 17 out of 28 children made *significant* growth across the four testing events in one or more of the seven dependent measures. Table 4.1 shows the growth profile of the 17 children displaying significant slopes indicating the area of language performance in which growth was revealed.

We found it particularly interesting that 17 out of the sample of 28 students made significant growth in some area of JFL competence, but that the pattern of growth was not uniform across the children. That is, the children displayed varied profiles of growth in different domains of language use and knowledge. This finding is important to understanding foreign language development in the classroom setting because it indicates the inherent variability of development among students during the acquisition process. In addition, this variability characterizes the nature of individual differences in the foreign language classroom and the necessity of acknowledging the idiosyncratic nature of growth in classroom language learning across several components of target language knowledge and skill. That is, for the students in our sample, growth in one area of language ability did not necessarily predict concomitant growth in another. We also found it interesting that pronunciation, so frequently associated with advantages for the young language learner, showed no significant growth across 12 months for any student. Of course, this may be due to the children's previous strong performance in pronunciation and, therefore, reflect a regression to the mean.

The GCA also provides a window into program effectiveness and our monitoring and evaluation efforts. When locating growth density, we find that six of the children grew significantly in fluency and eight of the children showed marked progress in vocabulary development. This finding confirms that the program was meeting its expressed goals of increased target language production and vocabulary knowledge.

Documenting Student Language Achievement

Table 4.1 Significant slopes for seven measures on the GCA

Student	Measures						
	JPVT	C	F	V	P	G	Pro-I
S1			X	X			X
S2	X						
S3							X
S4		X	X				
S5	X		X				
S6	X			X			
S7						X	
S8	X				−X		−X
S9				X			
S10		X				X	
S11	X		X				
S12			X				
S13			X				
S14	X						
S15	X						
S16	X			X			
S17				X			

X: positive significant slopes; −X: negative significant slopes.

Moreover, when taken together, we find that only 10% of all slopes were negative for the 28 children across seven measures of target language proficiency. More specifically, this finding indicates that 90% of the children in the sample either revealed significant growth on one or more of seven measures of second language proficiency, although at a rate that did not reach statistical significance, or maintained their language ability over time. Students' progress in various and distinct aspects of foreign language competence was indicative of the integrative nature of the JFL program. Although no child made significant gains across all seven measures, each one of the seven areas tested showed development by some students in the sample. This finding is noteworthy given the goals and curricular emphasis of the program in the third year.

We also found that the growth curves for the two measures of vocabulary development (JPVT and the vocabulary dimension on the SOF) were not similar. That is, only two students among the 18 'growers' showed significant growth on both the JPVT and the vocabulary rating on the SOF. This lack of uniform growth, ostensibly on two measures of the same language dimension, indicates that word naming on the Pro-I and word recognition on the JPVT capture two independent abilities in JFL vocabulary learning, namely, production and reception. Thus, the GCA allows us to see more clearly how growth occurs across and within features of language use and prevents unwarranted or erroneous claims based on a single proficiency measure during a single testing event.

Documenting JFL Vocabulary Development in Year 3

The JPVT was administered three times during the year to 195 students and consisted of 25 vocabulary items read to the students by the teacher who directed them to indicate the correct corresponding picture by marking it in their answer book. To this end, the JPVT can be seen as a measure of students' receptive ability and not necessarily their ability to produce vocabulary spontaneously during target language interactions. The data were analyzed using a three-way analysis of variance. Time of testing (October, February, May), age (older: grades 3–5, and younger: grades K-2) and gender (male and female) were the independent variables with repeated measures on the first factor.

The overall analyses revealed significant main effects for time of testing ($F = 179.61$; 2370 df; $p < 0.01$), age ($F = 4.07$; 1185 df; $p < 0.05$) and gender ($F = 4.58$; 1185 df; $p < 0.05$). Of the possible interactions, only the two-way interaction involving grade and time of testing was significant ($F = 4.28$; 2370 df; $p < 0.01$). What the data reveal essentially is that the girls ($x = 16.25$) on average performed better than the boys ($x = 15.57$); the older youngsters (i.e. those in grades 3–5) performed better ($x = 16.25$) than the younger ($x = 15.55$); and the students demonstrated progress during the year from the October testing ($x = 13.29$) to February ($x = 17.12$) to May ($x = 17.34$). For the most part, the differences within groups were small and probably not educationally significant. However, there was a pattern of sharp growth from the beginning to the middle of the year that may reflect a resurgence of progress by students in Japanese following the beginning of classes again after the long summer recess.

The significant two-way interaction of age by time of testing was particularly interesting. An examination of the means reveals that the pattern of receptive vocabulary growth for the young students (grades K-2) is steeper than that for the older youngsters. The young students who perform less well ($x = 12.71$) than the older students ($x = 13.85$) actually outperform them on the end-of-year test administration (young $x = 17.41$; older $x = 17.28$). Thus, we can conclude that the younger students are not at all disadvantaged because of their age when compared with older learners on measures of receptive vocabulary. In year three, we see an equalization of performance and clear indications that younger learners are performing on par – if not slightly better than – their older counterparts. This lack of disadvantage for younger learners was reinforced when we examined total number of years in the program. A comparison of grade 2 children who had been in the program for three years ($x = 16.36$) indicates that they performed similarly to fifth graders who have also been in the program for three years ($x = 16.77$). Thus, in addition to having more positive attitudes toward language learning, another advantage of an early start, as we have argued elsewhere (Donato et al., 1994), is that younger learners perform as well as, if not occasionally better than, older children in elementary school.

Three-year JFL summary

The data on the linguistic achievement of these children after three years or 135 hours of instruction revealed a steady growth in their ability to express themselves verbally, acquire vocabulary and expand their control of specific syntactic features of Japanese. Over the first three years of the program, we found that the children in our sample were moving upward along the proficiency continuum from primarily comprehension skills to the production of formulaic speech to creative output. Additionally, this growth in oral language proficiency was accompanied by significant growth in several dimensions of language use as indicated by the GCA. Although no child presented exactly the same profile of linguistic growth, a majority of the children in the sample displayed statistically significant improvement in one or more dimensions of linguistic ability. Closer analysis of the Pro-I data also showed that children moved from word to phrase to sentence level production, controlled yes-no questions before wh- questions, and hypothesized about and used particles during speaking tasks. The comparative data for younger versus older students also indicate that the older outperformed the younger on some tasks, but that younger students were no less able to acquire language and vocabulary at comparable rates and with similar patterns of growth. This finding casts some doubt on the unquestioned assumption that older students (grades 3–5) are categorically equipped to learn foreign languages in the classroom better than the younger students (grades K-2). At the conclusion of year 3, we believed that foreign language instruction in the elementary school can make important and long overdue contributions to the cultural and linguistic development of elementary school children.

Students' Cumulative Oral Language Development: Year 6 of JFL

During year 6 of the JFL program, we continued our longitudinal assessment of a cohort of 31 students in grades 4 and 5 who had participated in the program since kindergarten. Oral interviews were administered in late May 1998. We continued to use the Pro-I so that their performance could be compared with that of other groups of students. These fourth- and fifth-grade children had been with the program since its inception and had studied Japanese for five and six years, respectively.

Each student was interviewed by a trained native speaker of Japanese following a standard pre-tested protocol in which a variety of tasks were used to elicit samples of Japanese from the student (e.g. general greetings and warm up), a set of elicited repetition items presented in Japanese (e.g. drank, drank orange juice, drank delicious orange juice, Dad and Mom drank delicious orange juice), a set of grammaticality judgments in which the pupil had to choose which of two alternatives sounded 'better', several sets of questions keyed to a set of colorful pictures that the children looked at (e.g. forced-choice yes/no and true/false questions; and open ended wh- questions) and a picture narration task in which the student was asked to tell a story about a sequence of six pictures depicting a typical morning of Kerrog the frog, a classroom puppet with whom the children were familiar. New to our interview format in year 6 was a grammaticality judgment task and storytelling task. The interview concluded with a wrap-up session in which the pupil was asked to read in Japanese a series of numbers printed in kanji. It was clear to us that as our research grew and we learned more about what these children could do, we needed to expand our assessment procedures to capture more of the children's emerging abilities in more finely tuned ways.

Table 4.2 Pro-I ratings for grade 4 and grade 5 children

Rating	Grade 4 (n =11)	Grade 5 (n =20)	Total (n =31)
IL	1	1	
NH	7	9	16
NM	1	4	5
NL	3	6	9

N and I: novice and intermediate level proficiency; L, M and H: low, mid and high.

Interview sessions were video- or audio-recorded and lasted approximately 15 minutes. Another trained native-speaker observer assessed the child's performance and assigned a 'global' rating to the student's oral production (e.g. novice-low, intermediate-mid, etc.) guided by a scale developed by staff at the Center for Applied Linguistics adapted from the ACTFL oral proficiency rating scale. A Japanese testing coordinator oversaw all interviews and independently rated approximately 50% of the interviews with an inter-rater reliability of 100%.

The results of the Pro-I global assessment are presented in Table 4.2. A majority of the children (52%) were judged to be at the novice-high level (grade 4 = 63%; grade 5 = 46%). Five of the grade 5 children (25%) were judged to be at either the novice-high or intermediate-low level while only one of the grade 4 pupils (9%) was assessed at this level. The remaining nine pupils were judged to be at the novice-low level.

Longitudinal perspectives on proficiency

For illustrative purposes, we compare results from year 6 testing to the performance of the pupils tested in 1993, 1994 and 1995. By looking across six years of instruction, it appears that the children were making progress, although the majority of them were still performing within the novice range. Table 4.3 summarizes student cumulative oral language performance across six years of instruction.

Given the lack of longitudinal data on the foreign language development of students who have participated in early language learning programs of similar duration and instructional approach, it is difficult to determine whether the children's oral language development was progressing at an acceptable rate for the number of contact hours and for the type of instruction they had received. What can be determined from these data, however, is that the children exhibited the ability to

Table 4.3 Pro-I ratings for the cohort across time

Rating	1993 (n =32)	1994 (n =36)	1995 (n =42)	1998 (n =31)
IL	1	2	1	
IL/NH	1			
NH	2	3	2	5
NMH	2	2	8	
NM	6	11	12	16
NML	4	12	11	
NL	16	7	4	9
NLL	2	2		

N and I: novice and intermediate level proficiency; L, M and H: low, mid and high.

perform Pro-I tasks at higher levels than in previous years and that they were clearly advancing on the proficiency scale. If these children are typical elementary school students, and there is no reason to believe otherwise, then these data suggest that overly enthusiastic expectations for language development in sequential early language learning programs must be tempered with the realization that to progress through various stages of novice-level performance, children require a good deal of time on task. These empirical data also corroborate and confirm professional opinion in the ACTFL performance guidelines for K-12 learners (Swender & Duncan, 1998). According to the performance guidelines, in K-8 sequences of instruction, children are expected to achieve intermediate-mid proficiency by the conclusion of their study. The cohort students in their fifth or sixth year of study appear, therefore, to have achieved levels of performance as anticipated and predicted by the architects of the guidelines; that is, novice and intermediate levels of proficiency with no student approaching pre-advanced performance.

Summary of cumulative oral language development over six years of JFL

We have documented that after five and six years of instruction, most students score within the novice level on proficiency interviews. One might expect that, after six years of instruction, some students would be scoring well into the intermediate range of proficiency. Are these novice ratings a function of the students' limited time on task (i.e.

classroom instruction of only 15 minutes per day five days per week), the teacher's expectations concerning the students' language development, the content of the lessons themselves, the teacher's patterns of classroom language use, or the frequency of opportunities afforded to students for extended language production, such as in story retelling tasks? Do these results suggest the necessity to temper typical expectations about progress that students participating in early language learning programs are likely to make, as shown by the results of four administrations of the Pro-I after six years of instruction? Thus, a critical issue to understanding foreign language development in the young learner is that children appear to advance slowly through the novice performance range and may only reach intermediate levels of performance long after the onset of study. From another perspective, this finding might point to the inevitable conclusion that, for children to make substantive progress in their language development, the instructional period allocated to foreign languages needs to be lengthened.

Another important and related issue is to re-examine closely the instructional approaches used in early language learner programs and ask whether it would be possible for children to progress more quickly if teaching practice were different. What are the implications of our findings that the students examined in this JFL program, although demonstrating solid lexical knowledge of Japanese, rarely demonstrated the ability to engage in unplanned, interpersonal communication and were not able to produce language beyond isolated words and sentences? These findings raise important implications for the form and the content of instruction. We have seen that a curriculum based on contextualization and culture does not necessarily lead to language creativity; and classroom interaction between students and teachers does not categorically promote autonomous, interpersonal communication skills. Thus, a critical issue to be addressed in the future is why does so little creative language and interpersonal communication occur in early language learning classes, and is this observed pattern typical of other early foreign language classes across the country? This issue might lead to a reconsideration of how we educate foreign language teachers of young children and how we communicate our expectations for children's performance, the contents of the curriculum and the instructional tasks and classroom talk during instruction.

Although students made clear progress in the six years of our work on assessing oral language development, we must point out that our expectations were misaligned with actual performance. Justifying an early start based on assumptions that children will make rapid progress in language development in contrast to beginning instruction in middle school or high school seems misguided. Language learning takes time and this is seen dramatically in young children. As we will explain in later chapters, the Japanese program was not sustainable in this school and was discontinued in 2005. We must speculate that part of the decision to close this program may have had to do with the fact that these children did not seem to be making substantive progress in their Japanese language development or were not perceived to be advancing in their language learning. However, as we learn more about foreign language development and understand better what progress can realistically be made, those responsible for early foreign language learning programs might be better equipped to judge the quality of programs and the achievement of their students.

Students' Spanish Literacy Development over Time

As work progressed on the documentation of student language development, the Spanish program provided a unique opportunity to examine the Spanish writing ability of the students. As we previously mentioned, the Japanese program emphasized spoken language and comprehension, thus the learning of Japanese syllabaries and Kanji were not the focus of instruction and did not figure in our assessment practices. Conversely, the Spanish program, with its emphasis on academic content as core material for developing language proficiency in grades 6–8, provided us with the occasion to document over time the literacy achievement of students in the middle school. To this end, we collected and analyzed writing samples of five students in grade 6 and again in grade 8. These students were the only members of the original cohort of 44 students who began the program in kindergarten and for whom we had a *complete* set of data for comparison purposes. Additionally, we were able to compare the performance of these students to a newcomer who entered the program in grade 6. In this way, we were able to examine differences between those students who had been with the program from its inception and a student who began his study of Spanish in middle school. Although the number of participants was small, we knew that we had a unique opportunity to examine and analyze in a detailed way students' written, personal and expository texts.

Spanish writing assessments

The writing assessments, developed through collaboration with the teachers and the partnering university researchers, included prompts explicitly related to the content and language taught at each grade level. In grade 6, the task directed students to write a letter to the Environmental Protection Agency discussing and comparing various natural resources in the community. In grade 8, students were prompted to write a letter to a friend who lives in a Spanish-speaking country. introducing the friend to the community in which the child lived. Although the two writing tasks represented different genres, our analysis allowed us to uncover important aspects of how early language learners progressed in their ability to engage in presentational forms of communication.

Writing assessments: Rubric scoring

Each student's writing was evaluated by two raters using a modified version of the ACTFL rubric for presentational mode of communication (Glisan et al., 2003) for intermediate learners. Student writing was scored on the following categories: language function, text type, impact, vocabulary, comprehensibility and language control. Each of the six components was assigned a score ranging from 0 to 3. Two raters evaluated the 12 writing samples individually, compared scores and established agreement on the scores of the 12 assessments.

For the *language function* criterion, each student's writing was assessed in terms of ability to describe, compare, elaborate, and begin to use connectors such as 'porque' [because] and 'pero' [but]. In looking at *text type* and *impact*, the writing was assessed for quantity of sentences, organization of the language, examples of varied sentence structure and attention to audience. For *vocabulary*, raters assessed students' appropriate use of the words provided and their attempt to include additional related vocabulary and phrases. With reference to *comprehensibility*, student writing was examined for the ease with which it could be understood by an individual unaccustomed to the writing of language learners. Finally, *language control* was assessed by analyzing the grammatical accuracy of descriptions, comparative structures, negative sentences, gender and number agreement of adjectives, and verb tense. The specific features of Spanish that were assigned to these categories derived from the grammatical features necessary for the writing task.

Using the results of scoring with this rubric, we looked at the end-of-year assessments in three ways. First, the rating for each of the six components was added together to produce a composite score for each of the six students, ranging from 0 to 18. Composite scores were divided into four categories and assigned a global descriptor: (a) exceeds expectations (15–18), (b) strongly meets expectations (9–14), (c) weakly meets expectations (4–8) and (d) does not meet expectations (0–3). The number of students who fell into each of the four categories for each year was determined, and comparisons on these global descriptions were made over time (i.e. students' performance in grade 6 versus grade 8).

Writing assessments: Analysis of writing functions

In addition to evaluating each student's writing on a global level according to the modified ACTFL rubric, an analysis of functions was conducted to examine language production in more detail. To carry out this analysis of language use, Halliday's (1975) *Seven Functions of Language*, was applied to each of the student writing samples. For this analysis, each writing sample was divided into idea units. An idea unit was considered as one clause governed by a single verb. In cases of compound sentences using 'y' [and] and 'pero' [but], two idea units were counted. After each writing sample was divided into idea units, the number of units was totaled and then each was coded following Halliday's framework. To establish consistency within the coding, two raters totaled and coded the idea units included in each student's writing.

Each idea unit was coded as one of the following functions: (1) an instrumental function, one that satisfies needs and desires, or makes requests; (2) a regulatory function, one that controls the behavior of self or others; (3) an interactional function, one that establishes and defines social relationships; (4) a personal function, one that gives personal opinions and expresses individuality; (5) an imaginative function, one that creates fantasy and imaginary worlds; (6) a heuristic function, one that seeks information, asks questions, finds out about events, people or things; or (7) an informative function, one that gives information about the world of experience. After coding several of the students' writing assessments, it became apparent that informative functions were frequently used for different purposes. Therefore, the informative functions were further subdivided into the following subcategories: (a) informative-comparisons, (b) informative-explanations and (c) informative-descriptions.

Writing assessments: Analysis of words and syntax

In addition to functions of writing, an analysis of words and syntax was performed. The total number of words, verbs, different verbs and nouns were calculated for each student's essay in grade 6 and 8. Next, the number of sentences was counted, and each sentence was coded as simple, compound, complex or compound-complex. Because the students produced a large number of simple sentences, the category of simple sentences was further subdivided into those that were organized in subject-verb order (SVO) format; those that began with a prepositional phrase (PPSVO) and those that began with a transitional phrase (TSVO).

Comparative results from writing assessments

As indicated previously, scores from the writing assessments were assigned a global descriptor. Table 4.4 shows the number of students in each performance category in grades 6 and 8 of the program.

As Table 4.4 indicates, we saw an overall improvement on end-of-year assessments when we compared the cohort scores from grade 6 to grade 8. Over time, we observed a decrease in the number of students in the lower ranges of writing proficiency and an increase in those rated in the upper ranges of writing proficiency. The grade 8 scores are particularly interesting given that among the five students in the cohort, four students *exceeded* expectations in their written performance and one student strongly met expectations of performance. On combining all students, both the newcomer and the cohort, all students are strongly meeting the expectations of the written assessment by grade 8 of the program. Interestingly, the profile of improvement matches the same upward trend in achievement that we observed in the oral language development of the children participating in the Japanese program. That is, over time, children improve oral and written ability slowly but steadily.

In addition to calculating a global score for student writing, students were also given a score out of 3 for each of the six components that were

Table 4.4 Comparative composite ratings on writing assessments between grade 6 and grade 8

	Newcomer		*Cohort*	
Rating	*Grade 6*	*Grade 8*	*Grade 6*	*Grade 8*
Exceeds			2	4
Meets/strong	1	1	1	1
Meets/weak			2	0
Does not meet			0	0

$n = 6$.

evaluated on the modified ACTFL rubric: (a) function, (b) text type, (c) impact, (d) vocabulary, (e) comprehensibility and (f) control. Table 4.5 shows the average score for the newcomer and the cohort of students.

By viewing the average scores of the cohort in Table 4.5, we see that students are progressing in all areas: function, text type, impact, vocabulary, comprehensibility and control. When comparing these scores with the descriptions on the rubric (Appendix A), it is clear that the specific writing skills are improving over time.

According to the rubric, a score of 2 and above represents student performance that is *meeting expectations strongly*. With scores between 2.2 and 2.8 in all categories, the students in the cohort show that they are able to (a) utilize the appropriate linguistic functions to address specific writing tasks, (b) develop writing that is cohesive and coherent using a variety of sentence structures and transitional phrases, (c) appropriately address an audience, (d) incorporate a more expansive vocabulary, (e) be understood by a reader who is not used to interpreting the writing of a language learner and (e) gain more control over grammatical aspects of the language. Although all the scores on the rubric increase, text type and impact represent the highest scores after two years. This indicates that students have more control in addressing an audience and combining sentences in a cohesive, coherent way. Conversely, they have slightly less ability with function, vocabulary, comprehensibility and control. This improvement is evident in Example 1.

Table 4.5 Comparative ratings on components of the writing assessments in grade 6 and grade 8

Criterion	Newcomer		Cohort	
	Grade 6	*Grade 8*	*Grade 6*	*Grade 8*
Function	2.0	1.0	2.0	2.2
Text	1.0	3.0	2.0	2.8
Impact	2.0	3.0	2.0	2.8
Vocabulary	1.0	1.0	1.8	2.4
Comprehension	2.0	1.0	2.0	2.6
Control	1.0	0.0	1.8	2.4
Total	9.0	9.0	11.6	15.0

Example 1: A comparison of writing: Dunmore, a cohort member
Grade 6 writing sample

En el foto la energia eolica es colares azul, blanco y neigro. La energia solar es mayor que el petroleo. La energia eolica es la granja. El petroleo es neigro. El energia hidroelcetrica usamos agua. Usamos la energia solar en la casa. Usamos la monilia en el energia eolica. En foto la energia solar es la casa blanco. La ciudad es mucho cochas.
[In the photo the wind energy is the colors blue, white, and black. The solar energy is better than oil. The wind energy is the farm. The oil is black. The hydroelectric energy we use water. We use solar energy in the house. We use the windmill in the wind energy. In photo the solar energy is the white house. The city is many cars.]

Rubric scores

Function: 1   Text type: 1   Impact: 1   Vocab: 1   Comp: 1   Control: 1
Total: 6

Grade 8 writing sample

24 de abril
Querida Susana,
   Hola, me llamo Alexis y juego futbol. Vivo en Pittsburgh. En Pittsburgh tenemos frio y calor tiempo.
   En mi familia es cinco personas. Es mi madre, mi padre, dos hermanos y yo. Cuantos personas en tu familia? En familia tenemos dos perros. Cuanto animals en tu familia? Mi familia es muy grande. En mi familia es dos abuelos y abuelas, cinco tias y tios y trece primos y no primas. Cuanto primos y primas en tu familia?
   Si usted debe vivir en Pittsburgh traer mas dinero, largo ropa, y ingles traductor. Segun escribe atras.
                                                                Tu amiga,

*[Dear Susana,
   Hello, my name is Alexis and I play soccer. I live in Pittsburgh. In Pittsburgh we have cold and hot weather.
   In my family is five people. It is my mother, my father, two brothers and me. How many people in your family? In family we have two dogs. How many in your family? My family is very big. In my family is two grandparents, five*

aunts and uncles, and thirteen boy cousins, and no girl cousins. How many cousins in your family?
If you should live in Pittsburgh, bring more money, long clothes, and an English translator. According write back.

Your friend,]

Rubric scores

Function: 2   Text type: 3   Impact: 3   Vocab: 3   Comp: 3   Control: 2
Total: 16

Example 1 provides the written response by one cohort student in year 6 and year 8. As can be seen in the student's writing, in grade 6, this student was able to repeat comparative phrases frequently. However, the paragraph does not show cohesion or attention to an audience, despite what was asked in the prompt. By contrast, in grade 8, the same student showed the ability to use appropriate functions in a comprehensible manner to complete the task, and to use variety in sentence structure, verbs and nouns with cohesive and coherent language.

Growth in student Spanish writing: Comparative analysis with the newcomer

Unlike the members in the cohort, the newcomer improves his writing in the areas of text type and impact, but lags behind in the areas of function, vocabulary, comprehensibility and language control. Table 4.6 isolates the newcomer's global score, and Table 4.7 shows how the newcomer scored on the specific component scores of writing. In the data reported in Table 4.6, it is clear that the newcomer does not improve in his global score of writing. He begins with a score that strongly meets expectations in grade 6 and maintains this same score in grade 8. Although it seems at first glance that he is not improving in his writing, this is not the case. Table 4.7 shows the newcomer's scores on the various specific components of writing. As indicated in Table 4.7, the newcomer increases in the areas of text type and impact, from 1 to 3 and 2 to 3, respectively. The improvement in his score shows that he developed the ability to connect discourse and present writing to an appropriate audience. Although he improved in these two areas, his ability to apply the appropriate functions, produce comprehensible text and appropriately control this language actually decreased in grade 8. He addressed the writing prompt with the appropriate functions, however he was

Table 4.6 Functional analysis of student writing

Function	Eaton	Keenen	Kohn	Goody	Dunmore	Rice
Grade	6–8	6–8	6–8	6–8	6–8	6–8
Instrumental	0–0	0–0	0–0	0–1	0–0	0–0
Regulatory	0–0	0–0	0–1	0–0	0–2	0–2
Interactional	0–1	1–2	0–2	0–1	0–1	0–2
Personal	1–11	0–6	0–9	0–6	0–8	0–3
Imaginative	0–0	0–0	0–0	0–0	0–0	0–0
Heuristic	0–3	0–5	0–3	0–3	0–3	0–4
Informative						
Explain	11–10	4–5	6–2	8–4	5–1	3–1
Compare	2–1	4–1	2–0	0–0	1–0	0–0
Describe	2–0	5–4	2–4	1–2	3–0	3–1
Total IU	16–26	13–23	10–21	9–17	9–15	6–13

Table 4.7 Word count

	Eaton	Keenen	Kohn	Goody	Dunmore	Rice
	6–8	*6–8*	*6–8*	*6–8*	*6–8*	*6–8*
Total words	127–213	86–136	70–108	53–135	63–104	30–72
No. verbs	18–35	11–18	13–18	9–19	9–12	6–10
No. different verbs	3–12	2–7	2–10	2–10	2–8	3–6
No. nouns	33–48	18–37	19–29	17–34	19–34	8–20

unable to sustain comprehensible and grammatically accurate language throughout the written text. This lack of improvement in functions, comprehensibility and control of grammar was probably due to the nature of the task. In grade 8, the students were required to *create* more with the language and *apply* a variety of functions. In grade 6, the students were merely asked to respond using comparisons that could almost become formulaic. Example 2 shows these changes in the newcomer's writing and his corresponding scores.

Example 2: A comparison writing in grade 6 and grade 8, Goody, the newcomerp
Grade 6 writing sample

El petroleo produce el plastico. El petroleo es peligrosos porque produce la contacminacion. La energia hidrolectrica no produce la contaminacion. La energia produce la electricidad. La energia solar produce el calor y la casas. La energia eolica no produce la contaminacion. La energia eolica produce eolica. [*Oil produces plastic. Oil is dangerous because it produces contamination. Hydroelectri energy does not produce contamination. Energy produces electricity. Solar energy produces heat and houses. Wind energy does not produce contamination. Wind energy produces wind.*]

Rubric scores

Function: 2   Text type: 1   Impact: 2   Vocab: 1   Comp: 2   Control: 1
Total score: 6

Grade 8 writing sample

Querido Quesadilla,
 Hola quesadilla de cuba, mi llamo es Joe. Yo pienso desde Pittsburgh Pennsylvania. Yo queren conto tu acera mi ciudad. Nuestra grande deportes de equipo son los 'Super Bowl' championes los Pittsburgh Steelers. Tenemos tambien Pittsburgh Pirates y los Pittsburgh Penguins. Tanto equipos son malo. Un fabuloso sitios en Pittsburgh son el fiesta illuminate en hacia al centro. Uno refrescar poner es Dave & Busters. Es un arcada y un bar.
 Que pasatiempos tu tienes? Mi pasatiempos son juego deportes con mi amigos y mi hermano. Yo gusta a comer y escuchar a musica. Que son tu favorite comes? Yo gusta pizza, sauce de caliente, y cebolla anillos. Que es el tempuratura en tu....

[*Dear Quesadilla,*
 Hola quesadilla from Cuba, my name is John. I think that since Pittsburgh Pennsylvania. I want to I tell you near my city. Our large sports team are the Superbowl champions the Pittsburgh Steelers. We have also Pittsburgh Pirates and Pittsburgh Penguins. So many teams are bad. A fabulous sites in Pittsburgh are the light party in the center. One refreshment to take is Dave and Busters. It is an arcade and a bar.

What pastimes do you have? My pastimes are playing sports with my friends and my brother. I like to eat and listen to music. What are you favorite you eat? I like pizza, hot sauce, and onion rings. What is the temperature in your...]

Rubric Scores

Function: 1   Text type: 3   Impact: 3   Vocab: 1   Comp: 1   Control: 0
Total: 9

Growth in student writing: Global changes

Referring back to Table 4.5, the ratings on the components of performance in grade 8 appear to cluster into three rank-ordered groups in descending order of improvement. In grade 8, impact and text type (2.8 and 2.8, respectively) reveal the highest achievement levels followed by vocabulary (2.4), grammatical control (2.4) and comprehensibility (2.6). The students' lowest grade 8 ratings, although still in the 'meets expectation' category, were in function (2.2). These pairings of improvement do not seem to be arbitrary and may well be a result of the content-based foreign language program in which these students participated for three years. In this program, teachers emphasized the learning of the foreign language in the context of academic subject matter where the expression of one's ideas, opinions and reactions was central; grammatical form was learned at the service of meaning making; and language functions arose in support of academic discussions. It is not surprising, therefore, that these students showed the strongest improvement in creating academic text types addressed to a specific audience (impact) followed by improvements in vocabulary, comprehensibility, grammar and function.

Clearly, the trend is toward improvement over the course of three years on the various components of the writing tasks. Additionally, we find that the rank-ordered rating of grade 8 reflects the order of gains made on the individual components of the writing task across the three years of the program. Specifically, the strongest improvement from grade 6 to grade 8 was found in macro-level writing ability, namely, text type and impact. The improvement of nearly a full point (0.83) on both of these components indicates advancement and meeting appropriate expectations of performance for this grade level. It is also not surprising that text type and impact cluster in terms of strongest improvement given their importance for a written academic text. That is, the writer must produce a suitable text type to address a particular audience, and the writer's understanding of his/her audience influences the decision of text type. Vocabulary knowledge and grammatical control exhibit the next highest comparative gains (0.50 and 0.33, respectively). Form-function mappings in producing written texts require both grammatical control and knowledge of vocabulary. Finally, comprehensibility exhibits the least amount of gain (0.17) across three years. It must be noted, however, that comprehensibility ranked among the highest ratings in the first year of testing.

In summary, students seem to progress along a continuum of writing development and show the strongest gains in creating a macrostructure of appropriate text types for an audience followed by moderate gains in vocabulary, grammar and textual comprehensibility. Ratings on expressing specific functions in writing remained unchanged and were in the acceptable range of performance from grade 6 to grade 8 (2 and 2.2, respectively).

Growth in student writing: Functions

In looking at the analysis of functions in the writing of the six students, several changes are evident. Table 4.6 shows the total number of idea units and the corresponding functions applied by the newcomer and by each student in the cohort. As seen in Table 4.6, all of the students' writing showed an increase in the total amount of idea units over time. The two strongest students, Eaton (this and the other names are pseudonyms) and Keenen, improved by the same number of idea units over the three years. Eaton produced 16 idea units in grade 6 and 26 idea units in grade 8, showing an increase of 10 units. Keenen produced 13 idea units in grade 6 and 23 idea units in grade 8, also demonstrating an increase of 10 units. The two weaker students, Dunmore and Rice, showed gains in expressing ideas over the three years. Dunmore used 9 idea units in grade 6 and 15 idea units in grade 8, showing an increase of 6 units; and Rice, another weak student, wrote 6 idea units in grade 6 and 13 idea units in grade 8, increasing idea units by 7. In looking at the increase in units over time, a clear difference emerges between the two strong and two weaker students. The stronger students increase by more idea units than the weaker students. This demonstrates that the students in the cohort are showing improvement in their writing, however, their improvement increases at different rates.

The newcomer also improves in his amount of idea units over time. In grade 6, he produced 9 idea units, and in grade 8, he produced 17 idea units. In grade 6, he is writing the same amount of idea units as the weaker students, Dunmore and Rice. However, by grade 8, the newcomer surpassed the two weaker students and produced idea units that are only slightly lower that the amount written by the stronger students.

A second trend that emerges when viewing a functional analysis is that the total number of functional categories used by each student expands over time. In looking at the types of functions indicated in Table 4.6, each student began in grade 6 producing mostly informative functions, with the exception of Eaton and Keenen, who included two functions, personal and interactional, respectively. By grade 8, all students, both the newcomer and the cohort were using four to five different language functions in their writing. This growth in the use of functions could be due to the nature of the task. In grade 6, the students were asked only to use one type of function, comparisons. In grade 8, the students were asked to write a letter, which lends itself to the inclusion of a greater variety of functions – regulatory, interactional, personal, heuristic and informative.

Growth in student writing: Words

Table 4.7 shows the total number of words, verbs, different verbs and nouns produced in writing by each student on their assessments in grade 6 and grade 8. In looking at the total number of words for each student over time, it is clear that all students increased their quantity of words over three years. Interestingly, Eaton, one of the stronger students, and Goody, the newcomer, are the students who increased the most in word quantity over time. Eaton increased by 86 words and Goody followed with an increase of 82 words. The remaining four students increased between 37 and 50 words in their writings over the three years.

If the students were rank-ordered as they were in the rubric and functional analysis, a similar order prevails. In grade 6, the students' amount of words produced follows the same rank-ordering as the functional analysis: Eaton (127), Keenen (86), Kohn (70), Dunmore (63), Goody the newcomer (53) and Rice, (30). However, when looking at the data from grade 8, the rank-ordering changes. Goody, the newcomer, produced more words than two of the students: Eaton (213), Keenen (136), Goody (135), Dunmore (104) and Rice (72).

Growth in student writing: Syntax

Interesting trends emerged regarding the students syntax development when we examined the sentence types that each of these students

Table 4.8 Comparison of sentence types used by each student in grade 6 and grade 8

Sentence types	Dunmore 6–8	Eaton 6–8	Keenen 6–8	Kohn 6–8	Rice 6–8	Goody 6–8
Simple						
SVO	7–7	1–10	0–16	4–12	4–6	7–15
PSVO	2–4	0–1	1–0	0–0	0–1	0–0
TSVO	0–1	0–3	0–1	0–0	0–0	0–0
Complex	0–1	2–3	2–1	0–1	1–2	1–0
Compound	0–0	3–3	0–1	1–1	0–0	0–0
Compound-complex	0–0	1–3	2–0	2–0	0–0	0–0
Total sentences	9–13	7–23	5–18	7–14	5–8	8–15

used over time. As indicated in Table 4.8, most of the students are producing simple sentences in grade 6. Eaton and Keenen, two of the stronger students, included six and four sentences, respectively, that were compound, complex or compound-complex. The remaining four students did not. When looking more specifically at the types of simple sentences that the students produced, it is evident that all of the students in grade 6, with the exception of Kohn and Goody the newcomer, varied their simple sentence structure by including a prepositional phrase or transition. Goody was unable to do this at grades 6 or 8.

In grade 8, all of the students, with the exception of Goody, varied their simple sentence structures and produced at least one type of sentence that was compound, complex or compound-complex. Only Eaton, one of the stronger students, included a compound-complex sentence – one of the more advanced syntactic structures in his writing.

Differences: The newcomer and the upper and lower cohort

Another goal of this phase of our research study was to compare the newcomer's performance to that of the cohort on end-of-year writing assessments in grade 6 and grade 8. First, it is clear that unlike the five students who began their study of Spanish in kindergarten, the newcomer did not improve his final global rating from grade 6 to grade 8 (see Table 4.5). That is, unlike the members of the cohort who all improved in the global assessment of their writing, the newcomer's global ratings across two years remained the same. Similarly, when analyzing components of his writing (see Table 4.5), we find that his total score in year 6 and year 8 remained unchanged compared to the members of the cohort who showed a noticeable improvement across all six components of writing specified on the rubric as well as on their total score for the writing sample.

A second comparative finding concerns the performance of the newcomer relative to the performance rankings of students in the cohort. We found that the cohort students differentiated in terms of writing performance. Although all students improved in various aspects of their writing proficiency, the degree of improvement separated the cohort into two categories – high achievers and low achievers. The newcomer's rating on various aspects of writing performance aligned closely with the performance of the students in the lower half of the cohort. Specifically, the newcomer's quantity of ideas expressed in writing paralleled the performance of the lower half of the cohort. That is, given the importance of quantity of production previously shown to be an important aspect in differentiating proficiency in the young learner (Igarashi *et al.*, 2002), the newcomer was unable to match the performance of the stronger students who showed gains of ten or more written idea units in year 3 of the study.

A third notable difference concerns the newcomer's growth in vocabulary in relation to syntactic complexity. One aspect of the newcomer's writing proficiency that diverged from that of students in the lower half of the cohort was vocabulary growth. In year 6, or his first year of language study, the newcomer's profile of vocabulary use in writing was quite similar to the lower half of the cohort. By year 8, however, after three years of instruction, the newcomer clearly outperformed the lower half of the cohort (see Table 4.7) in terms of vocabulary growth and he kept pace with or outperformed students in the top half of the cohort. The expansion of his vocabulary was consistently strong for total number of words (53–135), verbs (9–19), nouns (17–34) and different verbs (2–10). It appears, therefore, that the newcomer's late start did not compromise his ability to expand his Spanish vocabulary appropriate to the writing task and that he did so in ranges that matched the strongest students in the cohort.

Conversely, his syntactic development lagged far behind that of all students in the cohort. In year 8, the newcomer produced only SVO sentences in his writing (15 SVO sentences) compared to *all* other students in the cohort who were able to produce sentence types ranging from 3 to 6 syntactic patterns, including complex sentences with recursion, across 8 to 23 sentences in the personal letter-writing task. Additionally, the newcomer was the only student to write sentences that forced translation into English for their interpretation (e.g. *Yo queren conto tu acerca mi ciudad. *Yo gusta a comer y eschuchar a musica [I *want (3rd plural) *I tell *you (subject pronoun) *about (locative preposition) my city; *I like (inaccurate use of gustar) *to (locative preposition) eat and to listen *to (locative preposition) music]). It is important to note that no other student produced sentences whose interpretation relied on translations in English. This comparison indicates that in year 3 of his study of Spanish, the newcomer still produced Spanish through the process of relexification. By contrast, those students who had been with the program since kindergarten controlled the syntactic patterns related to the task of letter writing to such an extent that their written production never produced challenges to comprehension or forced translation into English.

The findings of this analysis of differences seem clear. The profile to emerge for this student is that he is eager to express himself in Spanish, attempts various language functions, albeit with awkwardness of expression, and that he was the only student in the entire sample to attempt an instrumental function in writing. The quantity of his written ideas is similar to the weaker students in the cohort whereas the quantity of his vocabulary expands comparably to the students in the upper ranges of writing proficiency. Where he differs significantly from all others in the cohort is in his inability to produce writing using a variety of syntactic structures, particularly syntactic structures with recursive embeddings. Here, the students with the early start have the advantage. We argue that the newcomer's lack of syntactic complexity can only be traced to his lack of experience with language compared to the cohort who had been studying Spanish for nine years. Despite the newcomer's cognitive maturity, his seemingly positive disposition as a language student and his engagement in the writing task, and similar curriculum and instruction over three years, his lack of early language experiences appears to have disadvantaged him in terms of his syntactic development.

Relationships Between Classroom Instruction and Oral and Written Language Development

After several years of assessment, we began to examine the relationship between what occurred in the classroom and the consequences of classroom interaction on students' language development. We carried out two small studies that directly linked classroom oral interactions to students' performance on end-of-year oral and written assessments. In both cases, we found a strong relationship between what was observed in class and what students could do with the language at the end of the year. This relationship also held between different language modalities. That is, we found compelling parallels between the quality of academic talk in the classroom used by the teacher and the students' academic writing ability. The two studies that we report on here concern quantity and quality of language production. In the case of the JFL study, we examined the relationship between the quantity of the students' spoken utterances during class with their ability to store in memory and repeat sentences of increasing length. In the case of the Spanish study, we examined the quality of the teacher's academic talk and the students' ability to integrate academic content with focus on language form and the students' ability to produce relatively accurate academic texts in writing.

Oral JFL ability and classroom practice

Observation data from the Japanese program were systematically reviewed for instances of creative language production following the operational definition we established. To this end, we attempted to develop a 'chronology of creative conversations' from February to May 1998 in grades 4 and 5. By creative conversation, we meant times where students were creating with the language to express their own meanings as contrasted with repetitions after the teacher. In terms of the national standards, a creative utterance can be viewed as uses of the interpersonal mode of communication. During one-fourth of the instructional time, we observed consistent language teaching practice based on professionally endorsed approaches to contextualized instruction (Shrum & Glisan, 2009). The teacher attended to binding forms and meanings through the provision of comprehensible input in meaningful contexts, often embedded in cultural topics. The teacher's lessons were highly interactive, keeping students on-task and involved in her skillfully executed, fast-paced activities. However, despite the myriad positive aspects of this instructional environment – contextualized practice, cultural topics, interactive presentations, engaging visuals, attention to form and meaning, and increasingly more complex language learning tasks – based on the data collected, we found only one instance of creative language use for interpersonal communication in the 21% of instructional time that we observed.

Sample classroom interaction

S1: Can you tell me how to say 'water' in Japanese?
T: Mizu.
S1: Mizu o nomimasu
(The student is attempting to ask to be excused to get a drink of water but produces the sentence 'I drink water'.)
T: Ie.
(A few minutes later, the student approaches the teacher again.)
S1: Mizu o kudasai. (Water, please)
T: Hai, Doozo. (Yes, go ahead.)

Of course, we cannot be certain that creative utterances of this type did not occur when observations were not being made of the class. However, it appears fair to assert that for one-fourth of the classes observed across seven months of instructional time, self-nominated, creative language use was rare or non-existent. This assertion, based on documented observations, leads to important conclusions concerning the nature of language use in an early language learning setting and addresses the concern that early language learners, whether in early language learning programs or immersion settings, may not develop into independent language users. Clearly, the evidence seems to support two conclusions: (a) contextualization and culture do not necessarily lead to language creativity and (b) interaction between students and teachers does not categorically promote collaborative interpersonal communication skills.

The source of this lack of language creativity in the early language learning context may be situated in the nature of the class itself, the developmental level of the children, the tasks presented to learners or the beliefs about language learning that still permeate the profession. Other possible sources that inhibit extended discourse development of children might be traced to the demands placed on a single specialist teacher who is challenged daily with presenting multiple lessons across a wide range of age groups and levels of ability. Adjusting the complexity of input demands careful deliberation and dynamic assessment of the class' level of ability at each instructional encounter – a task not easily achieved given the demands of classroom instruction and teaching schedule. Clearly, as Oliver's (1998) research has shown, primary school children ages 8–13 are capable of negotiated interactions in which robust exchanges to clarify and confirm meanings routinely arise between teacher and students and between students with each other. Two questions that this analysis raises are why, in this highly engaging class, did few, if any, real negotiated communicative encounters arise, and to what extent is this pattern of communication representative of most early language learning classes.

Relationships Between Classroom Discourse and Student Independent Performance

Given what we know about the discourse of this classroom, we examined the relationship between classroom discourse patterns and independent measures of achievement as documented during the Pro-I. We look specifically at two results of the Pro-I – utterance length during sentence repetition and the narration task – and show how student performance on these tasks can be explained by the classroom patterns of communication in which these grade 4 and 5 students engaged throughout our classroom observation year.

Pro-I performance and classroom practice

During the Pro-I, the children were asked to perform two sentence repetition tasks in which each sentence contained five major constituents that were presented sequentially and additively in the form of a backward buildup. Children were asked to listen to each constituent and repeat it after the tester. What is striking about the results of this test item is that the vast majority of students displayed little difficulty in repeating utterances up to three constituents long. As utterances grew in length (above three), performance declined dramatically. Table 4.9 displays the length of utterance and the number and percentage of children who successfully performed the task at each successive stage. Additionally, Table 4.9 shows that the children's ability to repeat sentences decreases systematically as utterance length increases.

More than one half of the students were able to correctly repeat sentences of three constituents of approximately three to four words. As the children were required to increase the number of words to be repeated (beyond four words), successful performance dropped well below 50%. This finding on a discrete task of the Pro-I can be explained by reference to data captured during longitudinal classroom observation. By the year's end, we documented that children, although engaging in more verbal interactions and increasingly more complex language, did not produce utterances in class beyond single-sentences of three words

Table 4.9 Sentence repetition task 1 and 2

No. of constituents	No. of children		Percentage of cohort	
	Task 1	Task 2	Task 1	Task 2
1	31	31	100	100
2	24	30	77.74	96.77
3	20	16	64.52	51.61
4	10	7	32.26	22.58
5	5	2	16.13	6.45

$n = 31$.

each. It is not surprising, therefore, that performance on this section of the Pro-I should reflect this class performance. All students were capable of repeating one-word utterances and close to half of the students were able to repeat three-word utterances. However, fewer children could successfully repeat utterances of four words or more (16.13 and 6.45%).

Storytelling

The final task of the Pro-I involved the students in a storytelling task based on a series of pictures depicting a routine morning of Kerrog the frog, a classroom character with whom the students were familiar. Six illustrations showed the character getting up, getting dressed, brushing his teeth, eating breakfast, saying goodbye to his parents and catching the bus. Four student narratives (two boys and two girls in grade 5 who were rated between novice-mid and intermediate-low on the Pro-I) were selected for analysis. The analysis focused on (a) whether the texts generated by these students were, in fact, story-like and (b) the structural characteristics of the texts provided by the four students.

For the analysis, Hudson and Shapiro's (1991) framework for identifying different types of narrative production was used. Hudson and Shapiro posit three perspectives from which to identify and analyze narratives – scripts, personal narratives and stories. Scripts consist of temporally sequenced events, often told in the present tense, and devoid of complication or dramatic tension. Personal narratives are first-person accounts of past actions where critical episodes and unique events are highlighted and isolated. Stories, among the most difficult oral texts to produce, are coherent accounts of unified culturally appropriate actions in which the teller controls linguistic devices to convey character, setting, rising action, conflict and resolution. Hudson and Shapiro have found that most monolingual English-speaking third grade children control all three types of narratives and that elaboration by the children within each text type was possible. The use of discourse markers is also relevant to the analysis of stories and demonstrates how the storyteller is able to bracket units of talk with linguistic elements, such as 'and', 'next' and 'then', to create coherent sequences of events.

Careful analysis of the oral texts produced by these children revealed that they did not narrate stories. Rather, the oral texts they produced indicated that the four students controlled some structural characteristics for script, such as the use of the present tense and the chronological arrangement of the events, but very few of the defining features of a 'story'. Additionally, no Japanese discourse markers were found in their oral texts, and only one conjunction was used in English (e.g. 'and'). Finally, no student was able to create a complication to develop a 'good story', although they could identify characters and describe settings.

In understanding why these children could not narrate stories from pictures, four important considerations need to be acknowledged. First, all six pictures represented highly routinized actions, sequentially presented in script-like fashion with no problem event portrayed. Hudson and Shapiro have pointed out that the best stories are elicited when the topic includes a clear problem to be solved. A script, or simple description of events, was the most likely type of narrative elicited by pictures of temporally sequenced actions with no clear complication. Thus, in the presence of better visual information, these Japanese students might have been able to tell a better 'story'. Second, since the narrative task was embedded in interaction, the children's discourse was often developed in collaboration with the interviewer. The interviewer was often observed to encourage student production and to provide solicited and, at times, unsolicited assistance for producing isolated sentences. More precisely, the interviewers encouraged the students to produce 'whatever they could say about the pictures' rather than assisting them to construct a 'story'. The result of this assistance was obvious in the case of one interviewer who was successful in making one student produce more Japanese, even though the student's random sentences did not exhibit any story-like features. Third, although the students could produce approximately 20 utterances to describe the picture sequence, the level of proficiency of the students may have precluded weaving these utterances into a coherent narrative with dramatic complication and linguistically constructed coherence.

Despite the above caveats, a plausible explanation for the children's performance on the storytelling task is that classroom instruction did not provide occasions for practicing this mode of discourse. On only one occasion did we observe the students listening to a story followed by one boy attempting to retell the story to his classmates. It could be posited that if children were provided with multiple opportunities to listen to and tell stories, they may very well develop this competence. From another perspective, in understanding the performance of early language learners, we cannot underestimate the influence of classroom practice on what they can and cannot do. As we have shown in the sentence repetition task, children perform in ways that clearly and directly reflect classroom practices (see Hall, 1995, for support of this idea). By extension, if the discourse environment of the classroom does not provide frequent input and output at the discourse level, then our expectations for students to perform in this way independently, and at a later time, may be misguided. In turn, when students were asked to assess their own abilities, discourse-level production ranked the lowest of all categories of performance. We see, therefore, three converging sources of evidence that reveal what learners can do with their new language – the nature of classroom communication, student views of their own performance, and later performance on formal assessment measures.

Written ability and classroom practice

In the Spanish program, we compared the students' end-of-year performance on a contextualized writing task based on the topic of energy resources to classroom verbal interactions during the teaching of the unit. Unlike our study of the relationship between JFL classroom talk and students' oral ability during end-of-year assessments, we now switched our focus to the relationship between talk and writing ability. The students were in grade 6 and had had a full year of Spanish taught through a content-based approach. We were particularly interested in how the two grade 6 teachers carried out this content-based instruction since it was relatively new to them and a unique feature of this program.

We had previously documented that the two classes that we observed had different orientations to the discussion of academic content. In one class (that of James – a pseudonym), students' attention was explicitly and routinely drawn to form. We posited that these students would significantly outperform other students on the feature of language control, specifically grammatical accuracy. Conversely, we believed that in the second class (Grace), where classroom talk emphasized the elaboration of a topic, various language functions, comprehensibility of oral expressions and rich vocabulary resources, these students should outperform their form-focused counterparts on topic development and academic content. What we discovered, however, was that Grace's students significantly outperformed James' students in every category of the writing assessment, including function, text, impact, vocabulary, comprehension and language control, with p values ranging from 0.001 to 0.005, as seen in Table 4.10. These results are particularly interesting since James' classes focused largely on language, but his students performed significantly lower in the grammatical accuracy feature of the writing task. Conversely, Grace led her class to focus on form as it emerged during discussion of academic content and as it was needed to express students' contributions to the academic discussion.

We find it important to note that in two different programs, in two different languages, and in two different language modalities there appears a consistent and systematic relationship between what students experience discursively in their classrooms and how they perform in the language independently on both structured (e.g. sentence repetition) and unstructured tasks (e.g. expository and personal writing). This area of research demands increased attention and identifies the critical need for teachers to monitor classroom discourse patterns, to provide regular opportunities to students to generate ideas in the target language, and to be aware of the consequences of ways of talking on how children develop and control the foreign language.

Where adult learners may be motivated to reflect on and consolidate their language knowledge at the service of using the language for their own purposes, children appear to reflect in their language use the

Table 4.10 Results of writing assessments: Grade 6 content-based class

Rubric categories	Grace	James	Test of significance $p <$
Function	2.2	1.3	0.001
Text	2.1	1.2	0.001
Impact	2.3	1.3	0.000
Vocabulary	2.2	1.4	0.002
Comprehension	2.2	1.5	0.004
Control	1.9	1.4	0.005

language conditions in which they have encountered the new language. Strong relationships were found between length of utterances used in class and what students could retain and say. Moreover, in content-based classes where students were systematically encouraged to reflect on form when expressing opinions and ideas, their ability to elaborate in writing with accuracy was superior to the class where emphasis was on form accuracy only.

Summary

With respect to the Japanese program, we ended year 1 on an optimistic note. The children appeared to making steady progress in their oral language development despite the relatively brief instructional time allocated to foreign language learning relative to other subject areas. The results from year 1 clearly indicated that a foreign language in an elementary school program of this type had the potential for developing language ability in young children much greater than might be expected from the FLEX models of language study that were so popular during this time.

By the end of year 3, 17 of a sample of 28 students made significant growth in some area of JFL competence. Children displayed varied profiles of growth in different domains of language use and knowledge – an important finding because it indicates the inherent variability of development among students during the acquisition process. Over the first three years of the program, we found that the children in our sample were moving upward along the proficiency continuum from primarily comprehension skills to the production of formulaic speech to creative output.

However, when we looked across six years of instruction, it appeared that the children were making progress, although the majority of them were still performing within the novice range. We note that justifying an early start based on assumptions that children will make rapid progress in language development seemed to be misguided. Language learning takes time.

With respect to the Spanish program, we focused particularly on literacy development, and we saw an overall improvement on end-of-year assessments when we compared the cohort scores from grade 6 to grade 8. Over time, we observed a decrease in the number of students in the lower ranges of writing proficiency and an increase in those rated in the upper ranges of writing proficiency. The grade 8 scores were particularly interesting since we found that students were at or exceeding expectations.

We also observed differences in the newcomer's Spanish writing ability. Although not the weakest student overall, his global writing performance more closely resembled that of weaker students in the cohort. Where he differed was in his vocabulary use, which expanded rapidly in his three years of middle school instruction, and in syntax where the newcomer was markedly different from all other students. Those who had been with the Spanish program from its inception never wrote sentences that reflected word-for-word translations from English, that is, relexified second language utterances. The newcomer would frequently convert English syntax into Spanish and lacked knowledge of parts of speech forcing him to rely solely on semantics when expressing himself in writing.

We also found a strong relationship between what was observed in class in terms of teachers' instructional styles and what students could do with the language at the end of the year. That is, we found compelling parallels between the quality and quantity of teacher and student talk in the classroom and their ability to orally recall Japanese sentences of expanding complexity on the one hand or the quality of their academic writing in Spanish on the other hand.

Notes

1. When reading this research it must be kept in mind that the research predates the publication of the ACTFL National Standards for Foreign Language Learning and the guidelines for K-12 learners. We point this out to contextualize our studies. After the publication of the National Standards in 1996 and subsequent revision and expansion in 1999, curriculum was developed and benchmarked against professionally agreed on goals and standards. What is useful when reading this research is also an historical perspective on the growth of foreign language in the elementary school and the issues, concerns and priorities that this research clearly points out. For example, it was commonplace among early language learning programs at the time to emphasize listening comprehension over production. Additionally, serious attention to literacy had not yet formed in the minds of those involve in these programs.
2. Although some may argue that the Pro-I cannot replace an actual oral proficiency interview, we have consistently found the Pro-I to be a valuable and reliable tool to conduct curriculum-based oral assessments with children.

Chapter 5

Documenting Language Program Development: The Views of Parents, Children and their Teachers

In Chapter 4, we documented language development in various modes of communication, over several years, and in two languages taught at two different schools. In this chapter, we move to another important aspect of the research – the feelings and opinions of constituents toward the programs. An important part of our argument concerning research with early language learning programs is the need to contextualize findings and situate programs in the school ecology in which they take root and thrive or fail to do so. Hamayan (1998) aptly describes documenting language learning in young children, and by extension, the programs in which they learn, as similar to painting a portrait of a chameleon. Any portrait of a chameleon is determined in large part by the environment that the animal inhabits. From this perspective, we also attempt to depict the contextual factors that are consequential to student learning and to sustainable or temporary programs. Attitudes and opinions are among the important contextual factors that the potential to have an impact on student learning and program health and credibility.

What Do Parents Expect their Children to Learn?

Let us turn our attention first to the question of parental expectations. In the following section, we examine parents' expectations concerning the language programs from a variety of perspectives. We asked parents in the first years of the Japanese and Spanish programs what, in essence, were their goals or expectations for the programs and for their children. Our purpose in asking this question was to identify parental thinking on goals for language learning, to determine if parental attitudes aligned with program goals and to establish a profile of expectations that could be assessed as the programs matured. To this end, at the onset of the program we asked parents what they perceived as important goals in a foreign language class and then at several points throughout the years, whether their expectations were being met. Let us turn first to the information that we collected from parents of children who were enrolled in the Japanese program.

Expectations and impressions for parents of Japanese students

During the first year (1992–1993) of the Japanese program, a questionnaire was developed to collect basic information from parents about topics such as their own previous language study, their encouragement or lack of encouragement of their child's study, their awareness of their child's progress in developing language proficiency and cultural knowledge, and their overall satisfaction with the program. Questionnaires were sent home to parents to be completed at their leisure. Seventy-three questionnaires (or 40%) from the 179 families were returned.

We examined with care the responses from 19 parents of the 32 'target' children whom we had earlier decided to follow over time (i.e. two boys and two girls from each of the eight classrooms that comprised the K-5 program). In general, we noted that the majority of responding parents (17 of 19) expressed strong *positive* feelings toward the introduction of a Japanese foreign language in the elementary school (FLES) program at the school and stated that their children expressed enthusiasm for the Japanese class at home. The concerns that were raised by the parents focused primarily on the limited amount of class time allocated to Japanese (e.g. 'the class seems too short to be worthwhile', 'my older son wants 30 minutes a day' [versus the 15 that were offered]) and the future of the program for the fifth graders (that is, would the program continue to the middle school grades).

One interesting finding concerned the parents' assessment of their children's ability in Japanese. When they were asked whether they could give specific examples of what their children had learned, all parents were capable of listing some of the unit themes or vocabulary of the class (e.g. colors, numbers, greetings, food, stores). Their personal assessments of their children's abilities ranged from satisfied for 15 parents to doubtful for only four parents. One parent stated that her daughter was 'excited about the words that she knows, and she's confident with her knowledge'. Another parent reported that her daughter 'has picked up a lot of basic vocabulary – colors, foods, family members, etc. as well as some rudimentary grammar'. Finally, one of the parents noted that 'recently at Epcot Center, the Japanese Pavilion was the only one that he [her son] showed any interest in and related stories from class as we saw things that related to it'.

Among the four parents who noticed no appreciable achievement in their children, one parent stated that her 'fourth grader remembers only one-half of what she is taught'. One wonders, however, how parents assess their children's linguistic gains – particularly in a language that they themselves have not previously studied. It is clear that the metaphor of viewing the cup as half-empty or half-full aptly describes the assessments of these parents toward their children's language development. Also implied in the variability of opinions is the need for early language learning programs to communicate clearly to parents what program goals are and what is reasonable and developmentally appropriate progress for children learning a new language. Lacking this knowledge, parents can easily withdraw support from a program based on erroneous notions of what counts as achievement and unrealistic expectations for what language programs can produce given the time allotted for study.

When asked whether they would enroll their children in Japanese the following year if the program was optional rather than required, the responses fell into four categories. Fourteen parents responded with a resounding yes, one parent said no, one parent said that he would ask the child to decide and three parents stated that enrollment would be contingent on whether Japanese interfered with other more 'important' subjects (e.g. 'I would enroll them if it didn't interfere with their other classes'. 'It would depend on what the options were. If it were Japanese versus study hall or recess, I would say yes'). One parent explicitly compared Japanese negatively with another school subject by stating that she and her husband were upset that 'their child lost (15 minutes of) science instruction because of Japanese'. The notion of the marginalization of foreign languages in the minds of some parents and administrators is a theme to which we shall return.

During the third year (1994–1995) of the Japanese program, parents were asked to complete a 35-item questionnaire designed to collect basic information on topics such as their previous language study, their encouragement of their child's study, their awareness of their child's progress, their support for the program through their completion of interactive homework assignments, their overall satisfaction with the program and their attitudes toward early language learning in general. Questionnaires were sent home to parents to be completed at their leisure near the end of the school year.

Parents of 69 children equally distributed across grade level (e.g. what we refer to as younger was grades K-2 and older, grades 3–5) completed attitude surveys (younger $n = 37$; older $n = 32$ for an aggregate response rate of 39%).

Language experience
The background information indicated that 93% of the responding parents had never studied Japanese. A total of 40% of the parents reported having family members who had traveled to Japan, 12% spoke languages other than English, fewer than half had studied a foreign language in elementary school and 94% spoke only English to their children at home. This profile showed that these parents did not speak languages other than English on a regular basis and were not particularly connected to issues of early foreign language learning. The parents, therefore, represented typical American family members relative to foreign language study, its use and promotion inside and outside the home.

Perceptions and attitudes toward the program
When asked about their satisfaction with the Japanese program, 99% of the responding parents expressed a strong desire to see Japanese continue, 73% were happy with the choice of language and only 2% were not happy with early language learning programs for their children. A quarter of the respondents expressed some concern about the limited instructional time (15 minutes a day). When asked to compare their attitudes about year 3 with those for years 1 and 2, 57% of the parents reported feeling more positive toward the program and some stated this change of opinion was due in large part to the talent of the new teacher. Concerning the goals for their children in a foreign language class, enjoyment and cultural knowledge ranked as their first two choices whereas fluency in the target language was *not* reported to be a priority outcome. This finding remained consistent across the three years of parent surveys.

We were also interested in knowing where parents situated foreign language study in relation to other school subjects. To our surprise, we found that these parents perceived foreign language to be on the same level with core academic subjects such as mathematics, language arts and science. Twenty-four percent of the parents placed foreign language in a category all its own and only 10% viewed foreign languages as 'electives', our initial hypothesis. Their serious attitude toward language learning was revealed in the finding that 90% of the parents commented that they had discussed Japanese with their children at home and that the tone of their conversations with their children was consistently positive. This attitude represented a change in attitude from year 1, when some parents clearly perceived Japanese as interfering with the learning of other important subjects or competing with recess.

Parental perspectives

The parents provided two perspectives concerning early language learning. At a local programmatic level, these parents were satisfied with their children's language learning experience, supported the program at home and expressed confidence in the teacher. At a global level, the attitudes that the parents revealed on the questionnaire reminded us that parents may have a set of ordered goals for language learning for their children that may not reflect all of the proficiency outcomes of a program. For example, none of the parents reported that they hoped that their children would develop fluency in Japanese nor did they rank fluency as a program priority. Rather, their priority was for their children to enjoy learning a foreign language and to gain cultural knowledge. When asked to rank foreign languages in relation to other offerings in the total school curriculum, parents did not marginalize foreign language study or place it in a category different from core academic subjects. This finding was, indeed, encouraging for us.

In the sixth year (1997–1998) of the Japanese program, we asked parents of students in the fourth and fifth grades to complete a 23-item questionnaire designed to collect basic information about topics such as their encouragement of their child's study, their awareness of their child's progress, their support for the program through their completion of a series of interactive homework assignments and their overall satisfaction with the program. We sent the questionnaires to parents with stamped addressed envelopes and we sent a follow-up reminder to non-responding parents three weeks following the initial mailing. Twenty-one families representing 42% of the 50 grade 4 and grade 5 participating children returned completed questionnaires. Fourteen questionnaires were returned by the families of the 31 pupils (45%) who had been in the Japanese program since its inception and 7 questionnaires were returned by the families of the other 19 pupils (37%). Given the statistical similarity in return rates, we pooled the data for reporting purposes.

Language experience

The parents' language profile indicated that 95% of the respondents reported that they had never studied Japanese, but two families indicated having family members who had traveled to Japan. Twenty-nine percent reported that they spoke languages other than English, although 95% of the parents spoke only English to their children at home. Approximately one third of the respondents indicated that they had studied a foreign language in elementary school, French and Spanish being the most frequently mentioned. These parents typically do not speak languages other than English on a regular basis and they reported not being particularly connected to issues of early foreign language learning. Again, the respondents represented, therefore, an average American family relative to the study of a less commonly taught language, that is, a stable parental profile from year 3 data collection.

Perceptions and attitudes toward the program

When asked about their satisfaction with the Japanese program, 95% of the respondents reported that they were 'very happy' or 'happy' with the program; 81% indicated that they were happy that their child had a chance to study a foreign language and that the language was Japanese, while 19% reported that they wished that the language had been one other than Japanese (and they identified Spanish as the preferred language in the majority of such cases). A large number of the parents spontaneously offered the comment that the Japanese teacher was the major reason for the attractiveness and the success of the program. Given their overwhelming satisfaction with the program, 90% of the parents indicated that they would encourage their child to continue studying Japanese on moving to the middle school where the program was to be offered on an elective basis. With respect to class time allocation, 52% reported that they felt that the current program (15 minutes per day; five days per week) was about right whereas 48% reported that they would have liked to see more instructional time devoted to Japanese. None of the parents indicated any worry about Japanese study interfering with their children's study of other subjects.

The parents expressed clear-cut goals for their children in the Japanese class: developing an enjoyment of language learning and acquiring cultural knowledge ranked as their first two choices. Developing fluency in the target language was again not reported to be a high priority program outcome. Although proficiency was not listed as a program priority, the parents' serious attitude about language study was signaled by the finding that 81% of the respondents commented that they had discussed Japanese with their children at home from 'three to several times during the year', and all reported that the tone of these conversations with their children was consistently positive. These positive findings were also corroborated by the behavioral commitment of 81% of the parents who completed at least half of the interactive homework assignments with their children (see Antonek *et al.*, 1998, for more information concerning interactive homework). Among the parents responding to this survey item, 95% found the interactive homework assignments enjoyable and 100% reported that their children enjoyed them too.

Parental perspectives

The findings reported above for year 6 are consistent with the previous surveys of parental attitude that we conducted and indicated a positive and stable attitudinal profile for the parents of these children. What is interesting to note is that even after six years of the Japanese program, parental expectations of program outcomes remained consistent with previous years. This finding leaves one to wonder whether even in the face of interactive homework assignments, parent meetings, observations of children's performance in Japanese outside class and conversations about classroom life with their children, the parents' own history as language learners shape their expectations of the potential for language study for their children. What it would take to change this attitude is worthy of further investigation and may be key to understanding why certain programs are supported whereas others silently disappear without outrage or opposition.

Expectations and impressions of the parents of Spanish students

At the end of the second year (1997–1998) of the Spanish program (i.e. when children were in kindergarten and grade 1), a questionnaire was sent to all parents of first graders. The questions probed whether the student's attempted to use Spanish at home, the parents' overall satisfaction with the program, whether they made use of the telephone hotline, whether they found the Spanish progress report that was sent home regularly (in lieu of including Spanish on the school report card) to be useful and then asked for additional comments. There was a 43% response rate (98 questionnaires were returned from 230 that were sent home) with 99% of those responding reporting satisfaction with the program. Among spontaneous information provided were comments that the [first grade] child seemed to know and use more Spanish than her middle school sibling, that the Spanish program seemed to build confidence in the child to try other new things, and that the students enthusiastically enjoyed the program. Responding parents uniformly expressed the hope that the program would continue and described it as a wonderful educational experience. An overwhelming majority of parents (99%) also reported that they found the Spanish progress report to be useful – they felt that the prose comments gave them a better sense of their child's progress than a simple letter grade, and that it allowed the parents to know what skills or topics they should focus on at home.

At the end of the third year (1998–1999) of the program, a similar questionnaire was sent to parents of first and second grade students with a 57% return rate for the first grade parents and 32% for the second grade parents. The results were similar to those from the previous year with 96% of the first grade parents and 99% of the second grade parents responding that they were pleased with the progress that their child was making. In general, when parents provided open-ended comments, they expressed pleasure with the program, hope that it would continue, the importance that they attached to the 'cultural exposure' that their child was receiving, and their gratitude to the school district for implementing this program. Almost all respondents also stated that they found the Spanish progress report to be informative and helpful.

General impressions and expectations of parents

The general message that we come away with is that the parents of both groups of students supported the decisions to implement innovative foreign language programs in the schools. They were pleased that their children were studying Japanese or Spanish, although ironically they looked at the programs as a vehicle for their children to develop cultural knowledge and awareness rather than language proficiency per se. This should perhaps not be surprising given the location of the programs in what is essentially a monolingual environment where the students have extremely limited day-to-day contact with individuals speaking a language other than English. Additionally, none of the parents had experienced learning a foreign language in elementary school, and therefore held no pre-conceived ideas about early foreign language learning programs. Parents of students in both programs expressed an interest in their children's progress, a desire to be kept informed about program developments and a willingness to help to the extent that they were able to do so.

What are Students' Impressions of their Language Study?

We now turn our attention to the topic of students' impressions of their language study. In the sections that follow, we examine from a variety of perspectives, students' expectations and impressions of the language programs in which they participated. Our research benefited from earlier work by Robert Gardner and associates at the University of Western Ontario, who have developed a variety of instruments to assess motivation and attitudes of students at various age and grade levels (see, e.g. Gardner & Smythe, 1981).

Students' impressions of their Japanese study

In the first year (1992–1993) of the Japanese program, we developed and administered an age-appropriate questionnaire that was designed to provide information about topics such as students' attitudes toward school in general and the study of Japanese in particular, motivation to continue studying Japanese and the students' perceptions of parental encouragement for studying a new language. We developed three versions of the questionnaires to accommodate the students' attention spans and reading abilities. Of the 196 students enrolled in grades K-5 at the time, 169 completed the Language and Culture Questionnaires.

In general, the students reported that they enjoyed their Japanese class ($x = 3.85$ on a 4-point scale, $SD = 1.13$) and hoped to continue studying Japanese the following year ($x = 3.88$, $SD = 1.37$), but responded rather neutrally regarding parental encouragement for learning a new language ($x = 3.11$, $SD = 1.25$). When we dug a little deeper, we found some intriguing relationships such as a positive correlation ($r = 0.54$) between performance on an oral assessment and perception of parental encouragement as well as likelihood of continuing to study Japanese and perception of parental encouragement ($r = 0.52$). This relationship between parental encouragement, children's perception of parental encouragement and children's performance as well as their desire to continue their study is a topic deserving additional consideration.

In the third year (1994–1995), all pupils completed an age-appropriate Language and Culture Questionnaire in which they were asked to provide information about topics such as their attitudes toward school in general and the study of Japanese in particular, their perceptions of their parents' encouragement to study Japanese, and the importance of studying Japanese. The questionnaires for the K-2 pupils contained 10 questions with a series of four-point picture rating scales for responding. The questionnaires for grades 3–5 pupils contained the same 10 questions (and seven others of a similar nature) with a four-point verbal scale for responding. Grade 5 pupils also completed an additional section with 10 questions asking about their experiences in Japanese class, their completion of interactive homework assignments and their attitudes about interacting with peoples from other cultures. All pupils completed the questionnaires during class time near the end of the school year.

We were particularly interested in understanding student attitudes from two perspectives – the students' overall impressions in the *aggregate* (K-5) about the program and their view of themselves as learners within it, and *cohort* differences that existed between the younger and older learners. Our interest in the latter was part of the larger question that had guided our research with this program – when should children begin the study of a foreign language in elementary school?

K-5 attitudes

Of the 195 K-5 students who completed the Language and Culture Questionnaire, 85% agreed that they enjoyed learning Japanese and 73% reported wanting to continue their study of Japanese the following year. When queried about their feelings toward class, only 14% of the children reported some anxiety in speaking Japanese. Conversely, many claimed enjoyment in participating orally in the class (70%) and thought that 'learning Japanese was fun' (82%). Half the children informed us that their parents supported their learning of the new language by encouraging them at home and 72% commented that their parents actively helped them outside class. A chi-square analysis revealed no significant relationship between attitudes and gender, although female students rated their liking of school in general higher than boys. In the aggregate, it appears, therefore, that a majority of all program participants in grades K-5 had a positive language learning experience in the third year, perceived home support for their learning and expressed a desire to continue learning Japanese the following year.

Younger versus older cohort

A slightly different picture emerged, however, when the attitude data were disaggregated by cohort. A chi-square analysis revealed a significant relationship ($p < 0.01$) for questionnaire items relating language learning attitudes to perceptions and age. In all cases, membership of the younger cohort was associated with a more positive orientation toward the Japanese foreign language (JFL) program. No significant relationship was found, however, for overall liking of school. This finding does not suggest that the older cohort disliked learning a new language since 49% of the older children were found to be consistently positive about learning Japanese, whereas only 18% systematically reported negative reactions. What this finding does indicate, however, is that age, rather than gender, is related to attitudinal responses.

In the sixth year (1997–1998) of the Japanese program, we asked all students to complete a 31-item Language and Culture Questionnaire in which they provided information about topics such as their attitudes toward school in general and the study of Japanese in particular, their perceptions of their parents' encouragement of Japanese study and of the importance that they placed on foreign language study. Responses were given on a 4-point scale ranging from 'agree a lot, agree a little, disagree a little and disagree a lot'. In analyzing student attitudes, we calculated that scores greater than 2.7 represented positive attitudes and scores under this cutoff point represented less positive attitudes or negative feelings toward the response item.

On the questionnaires, we found that approximately 71% of the students, all having been rated on the Pro-I between novice-mid and intermediate-low (see Chapter 4), reported positive attitudes toward learning Japanese. The remaining 29% of the students, all in the novice-low range on the Pro-I, reported more negative attitudes to their language learning experience. We then compared the cohort students' attitudes (i.e. those who had been in the program since its inception or now 31 out of the original 32 students) with their performance on the Pro-I. A linear pattern between achievement and attitude resulted with intermediate-low students' scoring at the high end of the 4-point scale (3.53), followed by descending ratings for each proficiency-level below intermediate-low – novice-high students averaging 3.36, novice-mid students averaging 2.71, and novice-low students, expressing the least positive attitudes of the cohort, receiving an average score of 2.53. The pattern that emerged clearly showed the relationship of positive and negative attitudes in relation to achievement in these elementary school language learners.

Based on this initial analysis, we looked more closely at four specific items that directly reflected the students' attitudes toward Japanese. To the question 'I enjoy learning Japanese', 59.25% of the students reported that they had strong positive attitudes toward learning Japanese whereas 3.7% did not enjoy the experience. The remaining students were moderate in their responses toward enjoyment. Closely associated with the enjoyment factor and supporting this finding, was the prompt 'Learning Japanese is fun'. Forty-four percent of the students agreed with the statement that it is fun to learn Japanese, while 7.4% did not think so. When asked whether 'Japanese is an important part of the school program', over three-fourths of the students agreed with this statement (37.07% totally agree; 44.44% agree; 29.62% disagree; 7.4% totally disagree). Finally, we asked the students to consider their feelings regarding continuing their study of Japanese the following year. Closely aligned with the previous findings, over three-fourths of the students agreed that they would like to continue their study of Japanese in grades 5 or 6 (41.37% totally agree; 37.93% agree; 13.79% disagree; 3.45% totally disagree). Based on the relevant items, the students expressed positive feelings in learning Japanese, realized its importance and expressed their willingness to continue their study of Japanese. In the words of the students, they found their Japanese class 'fun', 'good' and 'happy'.

In the eighth year (1999–2000), information was collected by asking students to complete the revised version of a questionnaire previously used in years 1, 3 and 6, 'What Do You Think?'. We collected basic demographic information from the students (name, grade, homeroom, year of beginning Japanese instruction) as well as information about their attitudes toward the learning of Japanese. Information about student attitudes was collected in two ways: (1) by asking the students to respond to three statements (i.e. *I enjoy learning Japanese, I believe that Japanese is an important part of my school studies* and *I would like to study Japanese again next year*) using a five-point Likert scale with responses ranging from *totally agree* to *totally disagree*, and (2) by asking students to complete an open-ended response 'What three (3) words best describe your feelings about the Japanese program?'.

This information was collected from middle school students on completion of their second cycle of study. When the responses of students to the three questions were examined, the average responses for each of the groups hovered around the mid-point (that is, around the response *not sure*). There was a slight tendency for the older students to report that they considered Japanese to be a less important part of their studies than the younger students. They also reported that they would not like to continue their study next year (i.e. when they move to secondary school). This finding was ironic given the positive assessment by the teacher of these students' participation and level of motivation during class.

The responses of the students to the open-ended question where they were asked to list the words that best described their feelings about the program corroborate this relatively pessimistic finding. While a large proportion of the younger students use terms such as 'educational' and 'interesting' to describe the program, the older students use terms such as 'confusing', 'boring' and 'hard'. Clearly, there seems to be something about the cumulative impact of the program by the end of grade 8 that caused students to lose the apparent enthusiasm that had been characteristic of their participation in the earlier years (see, e.g. Donato et al., 1996, 2000).

We explain this drop in positive attitude and enthusiastic engagement with learning Japanese based on several factors that were specific to the JFL program. First, the single itinerant teacher was unable to easily articulate nine levels of instruction in this K-8 school. The default planning for this teacher was to recycle lessons, using the same core material across several of the years. What this type of 'survival teaching' produced was a repetitive content in the curriculum that differentiates across the years by grade level activities. Thus, students in the middle school might have perceived that they were not expanding their Japanese language and cultural knowledge. Second, when newcomers entered the middle school, no program for preparing these students to enter the sequence of Japanese instruction was provided. This lack of attention to newcomers complicated the JFL teacher's demands further by requiring her to develop lessons in the middle school that were accessible to all students, those in the cohort and the true beginners. The solution was often found in the recycling of beginning lessons that did not challenge the students who had been with the program from the beginning. Finally, because of the unique nature of the school, extracurricular activities (e.g. school musical, field trips) in which all middle school students participated and which required additional time in the school day were scheduled throughout the year. Often, the time for these extracurricular activities was made available by reducing the instructional time for the Japanese class. Taken together, it is clear that in a program where articulation and systematic time for instruction were often lacking, students' interest and effort declined and they perceived their language class as 'confusing, boring and hard'.

Students' impressions of their Spanish studies

At the end of the second year (1997–1998) of the Spanish program, a brief questionnaire was administered to all first and second grade students probing their ability to do certain things in Spanish (e.g. say 'hello' and 'goodbye', count to 100, say colors), follow simple directions, and ask questions as well as asking whether they liked to speak Spanish with their friends and in their class. In general, across both classes an overwhelming majority (greater than 70% across both classes) reported liking their Spanish class. The results were more mixed, however, with respect to their enjoyment when speaking Spanish with their friends (averaging only about 50% positive).

At the end of the eighth year (2003–2004), an age-appropriate questionnaire was developed and administered to students from kindergarten through grade 7. Among other things, the questionnaire asked whether they enjoyed studying Spanish, speaking Spanish in class and with friends, and asked them to write three words that best described their feelings about studying Spanish. In general, across the grade levels, the students reported that they enjoyed studying Spanish, that the study of Spanish was important and that they looked forward to continuing their study to the next grade. They used words such as *challenging, interesting, different, fun* and *cool* to describe their study of Spanish, in all a set of uniformly positive reports across the grade levels. A more detailed personal interview was conducted with a cohort of grade 7 students to probe topics such as their satisfaction with the program, their enjoyment in studying Spanish, etc. Their personal responses were consonant with the other questionnaire responses. The students reported that they were satisfied, that they were happy to be studying Spanish, that they liked their teachers and that they looked forward to traveling to Spanish-speaking countries. Unlike the responses of the Japanese students after eight years of instruction, the Spanish students retained their enthusiasm and enjoyment for learning Spanish. When we compare the critically important differences between the two programs (e.g. grade-level teachers versus single language teaching specialist, careful articulation, curricular differentiation and a regularized schedule for the Spanish classes but not for the Japanese classes), it is not at all surprising that differences would be found in student attitudes toward their respective foreign language programs.

What do Students Believe they can do with their Languages?

We now turn our attention to the topic of students' impressions and beliefs about their language proficiency. This aspect of the research was based on earlier work by John L.D. Clark and associates at the Educational Testing Service, who developed and validated the so-called *Can Do* instrument to assess indirectly the foreign or second language proficiency of students at various age and grade levels (see, e.g. Clark, 1981).

Students' impressions of their Japanese proficiency

A 'Student Self-Assessment' instrument for Japanese was adapted and designed based on the self-assessment instrument developed by the staff at the Center for Applied Linguistics (The CAL SOPA Student Self-Assessment) following the model provided by John Clark. This instrument was used in years 6 (1997–1998) and 8 (1999–2000) of the Japanese program.

In the sixth year, the instrument adapted for this particular Japanese class contained 11 items surveying the students' self-assessment of their comprehension (two items), production (seven items ranging from production of formulaic utterances to sentence-level and discourse-level expression), comfort level in speaking Japanese (one item) and cultural knowledge (one item). Examples of prompts included the following: *I can say hello in Japanese and tell someone my name* or *I can say how I feel in Japanese, for example, I am tired or happy.* Students were asked to select answers from three alternatives – Yes, Sort of, or Not Yet, response-types based on actual replies given by children when asked to assess their own ability.

A clear pattern emerged that indicated areas of student perceptions of ability and discriminated cohort from non-cohort students. In general, all students in both groups assessed themselves highly in cultural knowledge. This finding was not surprising given the strong cultural focus integrated into instruction by the teacher and, in particular, the year's class theme – the Olympics in Nagano. In addition to culture, virtually all cohort and non-cohort students expressed similar positive self-assessments of their ability on three language tasks, (a) comprehending commands, (b) producing commands and (c) producing formulaic expressions. Apart from these three areas (culture, comprehension of commands and production of formulaic expression and commands), differences were revealed within and across groups.

As JFL students were asked to self-assess on the production of word-, sentence- and discourse-level output, students' positive self-assessments declined in both groups with more dramatic declines reported by the non-cohort students (that is, by those who had not been in the program since its inception). Approximately 80% of the cohort group reported the ability to use Japanese words and sentences, talk about feelings and tell stories in Japanese, whereas fewer than 80% of the non-cohort students reported the ability to perform these tasks in Japanese. Moreover, comfort while speaking Japanese was assessed positively for 90% of the cohort students compared to only slightly more than half of the non-cohort students who reported feeling at ease speaking the target language. Thus, from the students' perception, both groups report positive self-assessments of cultural knowledge and the ability to perform word-level tasks. As task demands increase, however, the total number of students reporting positive self-assessment decreases with the non-cohort students rating themselves consistently weaker than the cohort students. One possible explanation for this trend is that the non-cohort students are slightly disadvantaged compared to their cohort counterparts because of fewer total contact hours with language learning.

In the eighth year, information about the students' self-assessment of their Japanese language proficiency was collected through a modified 16-item 'Can Do' questionnaire (Clark, 1981). The self-assessment had been pre-tested with several groups of students in Japanese and Spanish language programs during the previous academic year. The students were asked to respond to a variety of stimulus items (e.g. *I can follow instructions in Japanese, I can retell a story in Japanese that I am familiar with..., I can understand a story when told to me in Japanese*) that probed their comprehension and production skills as well as their ability to use language creatively. Students responded to each item by selecting one of the four alternatives that best described their ability (*definitely yes, probably yes, sort of but not totally* and *not at all*). The ratings provided by students in this type of self-assessment had been found in our previous research to correlate positively with direct measures of students' language proficiency determined by end-of-year prochievement interviews. Student self-assessments also correlated highly with ratings of student performance by the Japanese language teacher.

When the ratings were examined across all groups of students, a definite pattern emerged in which students reported that they were best able to follow instructions, understand names of things or a story told to them, and pronounce Japanese words and phrases the way they had been taught. That is, they reported that they could use language for *formulaic purposes* and they could *understand* instances of familiar or previously learned material. They reported, however, that they were less able to use language to *produce* – that is, they were less able to say sentences, to describe, or to make up and tell a story or to chat with a friend. They reported that they were clearly uncomfortable when asked to use language creatively at the discourse level. This observation, however, is not surprising since little of their classroom time was spent doing so. Clearly, the students reported that they were comfortable doing what they had learned and practiced. This finding in year 9 is rather disappointing. After nine years of instruction, one could hope that students would express more confidence in their productive language abilities. However, as we have discussed earlier, the nature of this program did not afford opportunities to students to build on what they learned in a sequential manner. By contrast, what is encouraging is that students expressed confidence in those performances that the JFL program could realistically achieve given the parameters of its operation.

Students' impressions of their Spanish proficiency

At the end of the second year of the Spanish program, an English questionnaire was administered to all first and second grade students probing their ability to *do* certain things in Spanish (e.g. say 'hello' and 'goodbye', count to 100, say colors), follow simple directions and ask questions, as well as asking whether they liked to speak Spanish with their friends and in their class. The students responded to a simple 3-point scale (yes, maybe, no). In general, across both classes the students reported confidence in their ability to carry out these simple language tasks or activities. In their responses to two open-ended questions, the students were also generally able to name at least two Spanish-speaking countries and to name one or more holidays that are celebrated in Spanish-speaking countries.

At the end of the eighth year, an age-appropriate English language questionnaire (adapted again from the work of Robert Gardner's team at the University of Western Ontario) was developed and administered to students from kindergarten through grade 7. The questionnaire asked what the students *could do* with respect to typical reading, writing, listening and speaking activities, as well as whether they enjoyed speaking Spanish in class, with friends, etc. In general, the students reported confidence in their ability to follow directions, to ask questions and to answer their teacher's questions. The students expressed a desire to be exposed to a wider variety of genres in their readings (such as biographies, scientific accounts of various phenomena, historical accounts, fairy tales, etc.). In general, self-assessments of their reading and writing abilities across a variety of tasks were positive (averaging 3.3 and 3.5 on a 4-point scale across grade levels and cohorts). Still, a large number of students expressed a desire to be able to speak more 'fluently' in Spanish while a surprising number expressed a desire to be able to explicitly translate materials from English to Spanish and vice versa.

Students' general beliefs about their language abilities

The students seem to possess an accurate and nuanced set of impressions about their emerging Japanese and Spanish language abilities. They report that their comprehension skills are more advanced than their production skills; that they have an interest in, and curiosity about, exploring other topics or genres in their new language, and that

Documenting Language Program Development   113

they would like to be able to try out and use their language skills in authentic settings. What is striking in both programs is that children assess themselves strongly in areas that are well represented and taught in the curriculum. Where time does not permit sufficient input and practice, children are tentative and less secure about reporting their abilities in these areas.

The Role and the Contribution of a Foreign Language in the Life of a School: Contrasting Experiences

Our work with these two programs documenting perceptions, attitudes and opinions of parents and students has provided an interesting example of contrasting experiences that may have implications for the profession. In the following section, we describe the ways in which administrators, parents and teachers can affect the implementation and the continuation or termination of innovative foreign language programs in their schools.

What roles do administrators and teachers play in program implementation and continuation?

The Japanese program and the Spanish program followed interesting, albeit significantly different, trajectories and may serve as interesting examples for discussion and comparison.

The Japanese program

The Japanese school conceives of itself as a center for inquiry whose mission is to generate new knowledge about teaching and to develop an inquiring attitude in students. After considerable study discussion involving parents, teachers, the principal and university education specialists during the summer of 1992, the school board voted to authorize and provide some modest funding for an initial three-year pilot program in Japanese for all children in the school from kindergarten through grade 3. Students would study Japanese for one 15-minute period each day, five days per week, and a new teacher was hired to provide this instruction. The school had not previously offered a foreign language program in kindergarten to grade 5 nor had it offered Japanese instruction at any level. In actual fact, much of the impetus for the program came from the chair of the advisory committee for the school who had recently visited Japan and viewed the establishment of a Japanese language program as a way to expand the cultural and linguistic interests and knowledge of the children and to focus their attention on Asia, which was rapidly becoming an important center for economic growth and development.

A partnership was developed between the school and the authors to provide assistance with professional development for the teacher who was hired and to conduct continuing formative and summative assessment. The authors, working with a rotating group of graduate students, initiated a program of research together with the preparation of regular reports that were shared with the principal, parents and members of the school board. Initially, the program fared well and became a 'model' that other administrators in the region visited as they too began to contemplate initiating foreign language study in the elementary grades – a phenomenon that was exceedingly rare in western Pennsylvania at the time.

When the program moved to the middle school (grades 6–8), a different curricular model was adopted – one that attempted to allow students to study Spanish as they had historically been able to do in the middle school as well as to continue their study of Japanese. Japanese was 'bundled' into an elective cycle with other subjects, such as music, art and technology, such that students who opted to study Japanese did so for a daily 40-minute block that lasted for six weeks and that occurred twice during the academic year (i.e. for a total of 12 weeks). The reason for this change of schedule was the need to include a technology course in the middle school that was deemed critical to the students' education to keep up with the current burgeoning emphasis on technological skills.[1] The result was the reduction of time for Japanese instruction rather than its expansion. Program reduction was further accentuated by the fact that the sole teacher of Japanese remained throughout an itinerant teacher who moved during the day from classroom to classroom, by the fact that since there was no provision for students who were new to the school, the Japanese teacher was starting from scratch year after year and grade after grade, and by the fact that whenever a competing activity occurred (e.g. preparation of the spring musical in which all students participated), it was the Japanese class that was cancelled so that the children could have time to prepare for the forthcoming activity.

The program, although it produced students who enjoyed studying Japanese and who made modest progress in their language development, never reversed course to become an integral part of the curriculum or of the school. When the teacher relocated to another city in summer 2005, the current principal suspended the program and commissioned a study to be carried out by teachers with input from the university collaborators to examine options for foreign language study for the future. Japanese was never restored.

The Spanish program
The implementation and evolution of the Spanish program was quite different. In May 1995, we were invited to attend an informal meeting with the superintendent of schools of the district and several of his administrative staff. The invitation resulted, in part, from our previous research evaluating the diverse aspects of the implementation of a Japanese program at the elementary school. This meeting was the beginning of a mutually beneficial and thoroughly enjoyable school district-university partnership that continues to the present day. The superintendent opened the meeting by articulating a vision for his students and for his district – a vision that included doing something different, something daring. He proposed that a new program be developed so that all of the district's pupils would study a common foreign language throughout their entire scholastic career. He described clearly how American secondary school graduates in the 21st century will be competing for positions in which numeracy, literacy, problem solving and communication skills will be increasingly valued and, moreover, how students with bilingual language proficiency will possess a comparative advantage in comparison with their monolingual English-speaking counterparts. He predicted that tomorrow's graduates would compete for positions in Beijing, Paris, Tokyo and Zurich, and not only for jobs in Baltimore, Chicago, Detroit and New York.

A number of questions were raised at the initial meeting. Was his vision plausible? If so, in which language(s) should instruction be offered? Were there teachers available? Would the community support such a program? Would the members of the school board support such a program – and provide the necessary budgetary authorization? How could the school district and the universities (Carnegie Mellon and the University of Pittsburgh) work collaboratively to their mutual benefit?

The group decided to form an 'Elementary Foreign Language Committee' to oversee the planning and implementation of a new and innovative foreign language program. The committee has continued to function to the present time, and consists in a typical year of the director of curriculum who chairs the group, the superintendent, principals from the elementary, intermediate and middle schools, Spanish language teachers from the various schools, the chair of the secondary school foreign languages department and the university collaborators. Over time, the university collaborators have included the authors working with a rotating group of students. The group meets to plan, review accomplishments and make decisions concerning priorities for future work. As appropriate, subgroups or individuals carry out specific activities and then report to the committee.

One key turning point came in the school year 1998–1999 as discussions began about whether to extend the program from its then-current K-2 sequence of instruction to the intermediate school (grades 3–5). We developed an interview protocol for intermediate school personnel intended to elicit their views or knowledge about topics such as the early stages of the Spanish program development and implementation and their views about issues likely to be encountered in the future with the imminent expansion of the program to grades 3, 4 and 5.

After consultation with district officials, we identified seven individuals to interview. Interviewees included four intermediate school classroom teachers, two administrative staff and one parent of a student participating in the Spanish program who is also a primary school teacher in the district. Telephone interviews were conducted over several weeks. The interviews were tape-recorded and written notes were taken. The notes were transcribed shortly after each interview. All interviewees participated willingly, expressed general knowledge about the Spanish program and reported that they looked forward to its implementation in the intermediate school albeit with a number of concerns described below.

As we read the transcripts, we noticed a concern on the part of a number of the respondents with what we refer to as their professional identity. Who are we ... as intermediate school teachers...? There seemed to be an implicit assumption that a successful intermediate school teacher must be a master of all the material that is to be imparted to the students. That is, the (certified) elementary classroom teacher is expected to have mastered a core body of material related to mathematics, language arts and social studies. Now, by extension, with the implementation of the Spanish grades 3–5 program, there appeared to be an implicit assumption that classroom teachers will have mastered or will master Spanish, as well. This assumption had important implications for the teachers' roles in implementing and supporting this program across the school and for continuing professional development activities. We noted that such an assumption did not appear to be central to the professional identity of secondary school teachers (i.e. a secondary mathematics specialist is not typically concerned with the mastery of a foreign language or with the physical or life sciences). We also realized that this assumption was not made by the elementary school teachers where the Japanese program took place. The sense of a shared responsibility among all teachers for knowing the curriculum marked a significant difference between the two foreign language programs. Shared and distributed responsibility for curriculum may be one important factor leading to sustainable programs, where programs, historically, have not been considered central to the mission of the school.

Several prominent themes emerged in the interviews across the seven respondents:

- Curricular integration.
- Full inclusion model.
- Time pressures.
- Teacher Spanish proficiency.
- Communication and classroom management.

The transcripts revealed a consistent concern of the intermediate school constituents with three issues related to the implementation of the Spanish program at the intermediate level: (1) what are we supposed to be doing; (2) when can we do this; and (3) how are we supposed to facilitate the introduction of this program? The consensus was that they were supposed to be incorporating and integrating the Spanish component into the core curricula of the school for all students. That is, the program was viewed (and continues to be viewed) as one that is central, rather than peripheral, to the district's academic goals.

Simultaneously, every respondent expressed concern about when they would find the additional time needed for the Spanish program in the face of an already full school day – one with teachers legitimately worried about preparing their students for the state assessments (in subjects other than foreign languages). The close linkage of the Spanish and language arts curricula may have helped to alleviate some of these concerns, but their importance to the participating teachers continues to be a factor and should not be minimized in this day of obsession with No Child Left Behind.

Finally, teachers wondered how they are to play an active and supportive role in enhancing the integration of the Spanish program into the core curriculum of the school inasmuch as they, for the most part, are not fluent speakers of Spanish.

We were able to view another 'window' into the role of teachers by virtue of a survey that we conducted in the ninth year of the Spanish program when we developed a questionnaire that was sent to each of the regular (i.e. non-Spanish language) teachers in the district. We collected biographical information (e.g. number of years teaching, whether they themselves had studied a foreign language), information about their opinions of the program, their thoughts about the students and their progress, and the ways in which curricular integration was or was not occurring. We received almost 100% return from the teachers. At both grade levels, the teachers were an experienced group, almost all of whom had themselves studied an additional language, with Spanish and French most commonly mentioned. Ironically, a majority of the respondents (67%) reported that they were not aware that the school district has a nationally recognized foreign language program. The fourth grade teachers responded that they made little conscious attempt to integrate their teaching with that of the Spanish teacher while 89% of the seventh grade teachers reported proactively doing so on a regular basis. The most controversial spontaneous observation by many of the teachers was their reported belief that students with individualized education programs (IEPs) should not be required to take a foreign language (as is the case in this district). At the same time, a large majority of responding teachers (more than 90% of those in each group) reported that they did believe that students derive benefit from foreign language study. We believe that such monitoring of the opinions and beliefs of the non-language teachers constitutes an important source of information for curriculum planners, and that data such as these should be collected on a regular basis.

Sharing information with others

Over the years, the university partners have assisted in various ways – participating in professional meetings such as the Pennsylvania State Modern Language Association (PSMLA) or the state superintendents annual meeting with members of the administration, facilitating participation by Spanish teachers in state professional meetings, participating in meetings of the school board as well as in parent orientation meetings. The Spanish program has truly become a university-school district continuing partnership, and Spanish has become an integral part of the school curriculum, obligatory for *all* from kindergarten through grade 7 and then offered to *all* children as an elective from grade 7 through grade 12.

The Foreign Language Teacher as Agent of Change

We encountered, and documented, a number of instances in which the Spanish language teachers became agents of change in program development as a result of engaging in collaborative activities that allowed them to appropriate a new set of instructional skills that they brought to their classes. In the following section, we describe one notable example with respect to the development of literacy initiatives in the intermediate grades.

Spanish literacy as a challenge across the curricula

Based on class observations conducted during the 2000–2001 school year, we noted that students were given little opportunity to read in the target language. In the majority of observed lessons, students received only Spanish oral input. According to the teachers, no reading comprehension was promoted at any level at that time. Reading in Spanish was understood as 'reading aloud' not individually but as a group. We were concerned about this because plans were well underway for the introduction of so-called content-based instruction (CBI) in the middle school (grades 6, 7 and 8) and the students would be expected to read authentic texts dealing with scientific, historical or other topics.

As for writing, after learning the Spanish alphabet, first graders started copying models from short sentences, while second graders wrote short phrases and sentences for describing pictures. Across levels, the Spanish curricula did not, at that time, contain explicit objectives for Spanish literacy. The Spanish curricula in grades 3–4 revealed no activities to enhance creative writing in Spanish according to the children's cognitive level.

During the school year 2000–2001, the Spanish teachers in grades K–4 and the principal of the intermediate school (grades 3–5) shared their concerns about issues of curricular articulation in grades K–5 with the members of the research team (and, in particular with Rocío Domínguez who went on to complete a doctoral dissertation on this topic in 2003). Their concerns can be summarized in three questions: (1) will fifth graders be able to read and write as expected in grade 6? If not, (2) how can we prepare fifth graders for a more rigorous content-based program at grade 6? Finally, (3) what steps are necessary in order to ensure the program's articulation in grades K–5 particularly with respect to literacy skills and expectations? These concerns resulted in a proposal to the Spanish program in order to ensure the articulation of Spanish literacy curricula in grades K–5.

A proposal for the Spanish program

The research team proposed to work collaboratively with the teachers to discuss and determine goals for reading and writing in Spanish in grades K–5 as well as to discuss with them the implementation of these goals with special attention at the upper levels. The fifth grade

Spanish teacher, a new faculty member in the district, suggested using an innovative foreign language method, called the PACE model, for implementing Spanish literacy in grades K-5. This model was developed by Donato and colleagues (Adair-Hauck et al., 2009) for implementing foreign language instruction. PACE (presentation, attention, co-construction and extension) is grounded in both Vygotskyan learning theory and a contextualized story-telling approach. The PACE model is consistent with theories that underscore the importance of meaning-making, authentic context and connected discourse in second language development. Thus, it embraces a CBI approach. This model stresses the importance of whole, connected or unified discourse as a starting point in second language development. Unlike skill-based models that fragment the language system by encouraging students to learn the grammar rules and vocabulary *before* using them to communicate, the PACE model encourages students to use language communicatively from the very beginning of the lesson. The model acknowledges the role of the teacher in negotiating classroom explanations as well as the contributions and background that the learners bring to the classroom setting.

PACE is divided into four phases: presentation, attention, co-construction and extension. During the presentation phase, the teacher uses a story-telling approach to introduce a text to the students. The main goal of the presentation phase is that students receive comprehensible input so that they can understand the meaning of the text. The second phase of the model, the attention, is brief. This phase is devoted to calling students' attention to some aspects of the language of the text. Whereas in the presentation phase, students are required to focus on *meaning*, in the attention phase, they focus on *form*. The teacher highlights any language features that are systematic in the text (e.g. specific vocabulary, subject pronouns). During the third phase of the PACE model, students, with the teacher's assistance, are helped to become aware of selected features of the target language. The cycle of the PACE model concludes with the extension phase. This phase is crucial since the teacher has to encourage the learners to use the selected linguistic features through a variety of activities. These activities should be oriented to promote interpersonal communication among the students while they have an opportunity to use their new skills. The teacher can also focus on literacy development by engaging students in creative writing projects or in reading comprehension activities. By the end of the 2001–2002 school year, the Spanish teachers were expected to set goals for Spanish literacy in grades K-5 appropriate to students' age and cognitive development, and to use PACE, a new method for them, to implement these goals.

During the 2001–2002 school year, the six K-5 Spanish teachers and the researcher met regularly, approximately once a month. Discussions at the meetings were tape-recorded and later transcribed verbatim. Teachers signed consent forms to allow use of the data. Meetings took place at the intermediate school and lasted approximately three hours each. Working agendas were given to participants before each meeting. The content of the next agenda was discussed at each meeting. Discussions at the meetings were expected to be a valuable source of data for understanding the teachers' perception of PACE. In response to the question 'what characteristics of the implementation of PACE led the Spanish teachers in grades 3–4 to adopt a new teaching methodology', the data showed that the Spanish teachers felt inclined to adopt PACE because (1) although they acknowledged some differences from their previous practices, they found PACE to be somewhat similar to their teaching, (2) they coped with the most difficult phases (attention and co-construction) with relative ease, and (3) both Spanish teachers observed positive student outcomes.

We found in this action-research project that outside change agents (i.e. the university collaborators) could play an important role in *making* the innovations more appealing. This study showed that when teachers were provided with different opportunities to observe, discuss and evaluate PACE, its impact on student outcomes and its advantages and disadvantages, they were able to appropriate and to use the model to enhance the literacy activities and opportunities for their students, thereby improving their readiness to participate in the CBI that they would encounter in the middle school.

Summary

In this chapter, we have examined the views of students who participated in the Japanese and Spanish programs and the ways in which they changed differentially over time with the Spanish students remaining engaged in their study and excited by it, while the Japanese students seemed to lose interest or become slightly less positive about the value of their language study.

We also found, to our initial surprise, that parents hoped that their children would develop cultural appreciation and knowledge from the early foreign language study, but not necessarily language proficiency. In retrospect, this probably should not have been surprising given the relative monolinguality of the communities and the lack of early foreign language learning by the parents themselves.

Lastly, we found that the Japanese program was essentially implemented from the 'top down' while the Spanish program was figuratively and literally implemented from the 'bottom up'. This difference resulted in one ultimately being seen as expendable while the other has become an enduring part of the school district's core curriculum – a theme that we turn our attention to in the next chapter.

Note

1. Interestingly, as will be discussed later, the Spanish program also revised its middle school Spanish schedule albeit not as drastically in terms of time as the Japanese program. The reason in both cases was the introduction of required technology courses with goals that ranged from learning how to type on the computer and understand the functions of the computer key board to using spreadsheets to improve understanding in algebra.

Chapter 6
The Sustainability of Early Language Learning Programs

As we mentioned earlier in this monograph, the two programs that we have been describing fared very differently. The Japanese program was abruptly terminated by the school's administration in summer 2005 while the Spanish program continues to thrive and be a source of satisfaction and pride for the school district, the participants and their parents. In this chapter, we wish to examine the differences between the two programs with a view to understanding the various conditions that promote or obstruct sustainability. We believe that it is important to examine the set of factors that may be *internal* to the program or to the school district as well as those that may be *external*. We turn our attention first to the internal conditions that create and pose challenges for program sustainability.

Internal Conditions that Create Challenges

We have identified six factors that create challenges for program sustainability. These factors are considered *internal* factors or conditions. We have tried to list, and then to describe, these factors in their order of perceived importance or impact. As we describe each of these factors, we will examine the differential way(s) that they played out in the two programs.

Decision making with respect to program implementation

The notion of the locus of responsibility for decision making for initial program implementation is, we believe, a key factor in long-term program success. We believe that it is essential that the various stakeholders – parents, teachers, administrators and board members – are invested in the process and have a shared vision for the program. The Japanese program was clearly implemented from the 'top down'. The chair of the school's executive committee announced that the school should implement a new Japanese language program and charged one of us (Donato) with developing the initial curriculum. The decision was made without consultation with parents, teachers or the school's director. The decision was also made to implement the program in all grades from K-5 simultaneously, and without consultation with the language coordinator for the middle school Spanish program. The net result was that there were no 'invested' stakeholders; there were no individuals who felt 'ownership' of the program. When the [sole] Japanese teacher announced in summer 2005 that she was resigning to relocate to the South Pacific, there was no groundswell of support to find a replacement for her so that the program could continue without interruption in the fall.

The beginning of the Spanish program was distinctly different. As we mentioned, there was a series of consultations by district officials with foreign language education specialists, a questionnaire was designed and administered to gauge community interest and support, as well as choice of language to be taught, and a decision was made to implement the program from the bottom up – that is, beginning with kindergarten and adding one grade a year. The district administrators, teachers, parents, board members and the university collaborators entered into a shared partnership with a vision that resonated positively among all the stakeholders. We believe that this shared vision and a collaborative build-up model of program implementation are key conditions that led to sustainable program implementation.

Situating the program in the culture of the school

From the early days, the Japanese program was a peripheral one. The children were not graded on their performance and the teacher was an itinerant teacher who had limited opportunity to interact with other teachers. At various times throughout the academic year, when additional time was needed to prepare for student performances or for student field trips, the time set aside for Japanese class was always the first to be sacrificed. When the program was extended from K-5 to the middle school, no attempt was made to integrate the teaching of Japanese with so-called core content subjects such as mathematics, science or social studies. Rather, the program (as we described previously) was 'paired' in a complicated and loose array of sequences with classes such as music and computers. This arrangement led the Japanese teacher to comment during interviews that she knew that Japanese instruction was overshadowed by the very subjects into which Japanese was intended to be integrated. That is, the primary goal of this loose scheduling was to ensure that special subjects were included in the curriculum while not sacrificing Japanese instruction. In the end, however, a lack of careful planning about how integration would take place and the role of Japanese in these special courses was never undertaken, thus Japanese never became a priority objective in the lessons. The reason for this lack of equity between Japanese and other special subjects might be traced to the fact that the Japanese program was never seen as central to the culture of the school. Except perhaps for one brief period in 1998 when the winter Olympic Games were staged in Nagano, Japan, Japanese was in the limelight largely because of a flurry of local media interest in the students and their studies. But beyond this one-time media frenzy, Japanese instruction was largely viewed as marginal to the curriculum, an imposition on the time for instruction in other subject areas and, as one student described it in one of our surveys, 'a commercial break from a regular class'.

The Spanish program, on the other hand, probably by virtue of its origin was seen as central to the culture of the school district. As the program advanced from primary to intermediate to the middle grades, the language teachers were given collaborative planning time with their grade-level counterparts. In the middle school, the program became one in which there was an infusion and integration of Spanish purposefully and meaningfully with other content areas such as language arts, science and social studies.

In addition, the Spanish program was celebrated with occasional presentations by teachers and students to members of the school board, as well as presentations and articles by teachers, administrators and members of the research team about the program at local, regional and national conferences and in various professional journals. The Spanish program was perceived by the various stakeholders as a critical part of the mission of the school district. Thus, when pressures mounted to devote more instructional time to mathematics and English language arts to ensure that students would be able to demonstrate *adequate yearly progress*, the concerned administrators looked for ways to increase instructional time in those subject areas without diminishing the centrality or the impact of the Spanish program. For example, in fall 2008, middle school Spanish will join several other subject areas in a four-day out of six-day cycle of instruction to allow for additional time for mathematics, English language arts and computer skills. Although some time has been lost, care has been taken to adjust the curriculum collaboratively by teachers and university partners to make the most of the time that is available and retain the content-based focus of the program. That is, unlike the Japanese school where the demands for more time for other subject areas resulted in a structural change, in the

Spanish school the change entailed substantive discussions and revisions to the curriculum to allow Spanish to continue to be a central part of the school day.

Teacher recruitment, retention and continuing professional development

Each of the programs identified and hired qualified teachers to staff the programs. In both cases, in the early years, the teachers were employed during the summer so that they could work collaboratively with one of us (Donato) on curriculum development prior to the beginning of classes. Insofar as possible, preference was given to teacher applicants who had both foreign language and elementary education certification – a consideration that seems particularly important as the program moved into the middle school with an approach that necessitated the integration of language and content. The teachers in both programs had a continuing opportunity to interact with faculty and graduate students from the University of Pittsburgh and Carnegie Mellon. The teachers participated substantively in regional meetings such as the Pennsylvania State Modern Language Association and the Northeast Conference on the Teaching of Foreign Languages and presented on topics such as content-based instruction and infusing literacy into the K-5 foreign language curriculum.

We have come to believe that the topic of continuing professional development is essential, and we continue to discuss this matter with administrators from the Spanish program. If the program, when it completes the transition to a full K-12, is to be one that will lead students to achieve demonstrably high levels of proficiency in Spanish, we believe that further and continual attention must be given to teacher development and growth.

Administrative staff stability

Each program has had both teacher as well as staff turnover. In the case of the Japanese program, a change in the director presented the opportunity to review systematically the overall program of language offerings in the school and to consider the addition of other languages to the program. The impetus for this review was doubtless motivated, in large part, by the fact that there were no true stakeholders in the then-current program. In this case, after discussion among the teachers and members of the executive committee, a decision was taken to eliminate the Japanese program completely and to institute a Spanish program from K-5 that would then intersect with the existing grade 6–8 program.

In the Spanish program, on the other hand, the retirement of the founding superintendent as well as the deputy superintendent for curriculum led to the appointment of individuals who saw as one of their charges the orderly continuation of the program and its continuing expansion into the upper grades. There was yet another transition in the Spanish school when the deputy superintendent for curriculum passed away in 2008 and was replaced by the principal of the middle school; but again, she had been an initial stakeholder who had believed in, and helped to shape, the program in its formative years. In contrasting the two experiences of these schools, we see an important generalization emerge regarding goals and priorities for language instruction. In the case of the Japanese program, goals shifted and priorities were re-established for other subject areas, leaving the Japanese teacher as a solo change agent working to succeed in the new scheduling configuration. Unlike the Japanese school, in the Spanish school, when the demands of No Child Left Behind (NCLB) created the need for more instructional time in tested subject areas, efforts to maintain the continuity of goals and priorities for language instruction were consciously raised and acted on by administrators, teachers and university partners.

Curriculum development and program implementation

The programs had one other interesting, and distinguishing, quirk in their original implementation. The Japanese program was implemented simultaneously in K-5. Thus, due to the simultaneous implementation of the program across all elementary grades, a continuing challenge was to differentiate and articulate the curriculum yearly for all grades to ensure that the students continued to expand their language proficiency, as they progressed from year to year. This was further complicated by the fact that the Japanese school has such a high student turnover rate that, effectively, the Japanese teacher was forced to begin each academic year as though she was starting with newcomers.

The decision to begin the Spanish program at kindergarten level and to add one year at a time to the program, on the other hand, provided an opportunity for gradual, carefully planned and well-articulated curriculum development. As the program grew, and additional teachers were hired, this also provided a cohort of teachers – some experienced and others new – who could work collegially among themselves and with other content area teachers to refine the curriculum. For many reasons, we would *not* recommend simultaneous multi-level program implementation. Our experience with the Spanish program in terms of 'rolling out the program' was professionally much more satisfactory and less complex than our experience with the Japanese program.

Need to serve newcomers to the program

The sixth internal factor that we believe to be important concerns what to do with newcomers to the program. The schools for both the Japanese and the Spanish programs are frequent recipients of new students into their systems; and the two have dealt with the phenomenon in markedly different ways. The Japanese program essentially made no special provisions for newcomers with the result that it seemed as though the Japanese teacher was forced to start over again at each grade level, year after year. The result was that the teacher moved to a thematic-based approach where the themes that were addressed each year were different while the language goals remained relatively constant and were modest to say the least. A by-product of this integration of newcomer into continuing students, according to the Japanese teacher, was that often classes were reduced to Japanese culture classes taught in English. It is not surprising when faced with such variable comprehension levels in a single class, that language use would be reduced to the 'language of wider communication' in the classroom, in this case, English.

In the Spanish program, on the other hand, the district has had three mechanisms in place to provide assistance to newcomers. The first has been an optional summer program of approximately three weeks in which students entering the district who have not previously studied Spanish are provided with an introduction to the language and the culture. In addition, during the school year, new students have the opportunity to participate in the AMIGOS program in which newcomers are paired with more advanced students who have been in the program since kindergarten who provide them with tutorial services. Finally, newcomers are offered the opportunity to participate in a study hall where they can devote additional time toward their study of Spanish. As our data in Chapter 4 have shown, motivated newcomers to the Spanish program certainly have demonstrated that they can keep pace, participate fully and do well in their Spanish classes, albeit with some noticeable differences in language development (e.g. syntactic development).

Summary

In examining the various internal conditions that create challenges for program sustainability, it is clear that the one with the strongest influence is whether there is, or is not, shared participation in the decision making about key elements of program selection and implementation. When the various stakeholders are active, informed participants, the program is, we believe, significantly more likely to be sustainable than when they are not. The Spanish program has survived to date despite pressures for additional academic accountability (more on this in the following section), system-wide budget pressures and changes in key administrators as well as teachers. The Japanese program, on the other hand, did not survive and was eliminated in 2005. We turn now to identify and discuss the external factors that create or pose challenges for program sustainability.

External Conditions that Create Challenges

We have identified four *external* factors or conditions that may, in one way or another, create challenges for program sustainability. We will describe these factors in order of their perceived importance. As we describe each of these factors, we will examine the differential way(s) that they played out in the two programs.

Pressures from NCLB to demonstrate annual yearly progress (in English reading and mathematics)

There has been continuing public debate over the past several years concerning the impact of the No Child Left Behind Act and its requirements that pupils in schools and school districts receiving federal funds demonstrate so-called adequate yearly progress in certain areas and meet federally established benchmarks or targets of proficiency by the year 2014. Issues of *Education Week*, in particular, are continually filled with stories describing the steps that many districts have been taking in an attempt to devote more time to reading, English language arts and mathematics. These generally include diminishing or completely eliminating the time allocated for 'special' subjects, such as physical education, art, music and foreign languages. Listservs and other forums continually share information about school districts that have eliminated these programs so that teachers can devote more instructional time each day to the subjects on which pupil, and school district, achievement will be assessed.

This approach seems to us to be very short-sighted in an era where there is increasing concern about the need to prepare our students for full and effective participation in the emerging global knowledge economy – an economy in which knowledge of, and sensitivity toward, other peoples and their language, values, attitudes and ways of life will be indispensable. Ironically, as school districts reduce or eliminate foreign language programs from the curriculum, students perceive that knowledge of languages and cultures other than their own is unimportant and unnecessary to their lives. As one student stated in a recent interview concerning the elimination of foreign language from state-wide graduation requirements in Pennsylvania, 'I don't think a language [is] as important to high school graduates as math, engineering or science – things you have to know in the real world' (*Philadelphia Inquirer*, 2008). Clearly, the move toward 'basic skills' brought on by national legislation and the subsequent implementation of high-stakes testing in reading and mathematics has produced distortions concerning what is needed to be prepared for 'the real world', resulting in an educational myopia in our children. The long-term effects of such short-sightedness remains to be seen.

Pressures from parents of children with special needs

The school district in which the Spanish program is located currently has a policy of requiring *all* children from kindergarten through grade 7 to participate in the Spanish program. This policy has caused some concern on the part of some parents with special needs children (or children with individualized education plans; IEPs). Some of these parents maintain that their children would benefit more from additional time devoted to reading or other language arts or mathematics rather than to Spanish. To date, the district has resisted the requests of these parents for exemption from the Spanish program, and has instead systematically attempted to provide accommodations for children with IEPs.

There is no easy answer to this general dilemma for, of course, not all IEPs are the same. The underlying condition in some youngsters affects gross motor control, but not sensory or auditory input or processing. For others, the condition may affect their ability to encode or decode verbal messages, etc. It is reported that only 17% of students with learning disabilities possess language-related disabilities, but many educators seem to think that any disability presents challenges to learning a foreign language. The variety of conditions is large and complex; and the extant research has by no means examined all learning disabilities to conclude categorically that all disabilities preclude successful and satisfying language study by children with learning disabilities.

One of our doctoral students, Heather Hendry, has examined the extant research on students with learning disabilities in foreign language classes and has conducted a dissertation study in which she has closely examined two students with special needs in a grade 6 Spanish class. Her study has shown that when appropriate accommodations are made, these students can progress in Spanish and that their frustration is reduced. However, as Hendry (2009) found, teachers are often unprepared to make the kinds of accommodations necessary for foreign language learning to occur despite certification programs that require formal coursework and documented standards of performance in accommodations for students with special needs.

Another major problem that has not been adequately acknowledged is that, unlike other subject areas, learning support teams and classrooms aids usually do not have knowledge of foreign languages, thus any interventions or supports that they can offer cannot be conducted in the target language. This leads inevitably to the perception that even when additional support is provided, students with disabilities cannot achieve in foreign language classes. The reality, however, is that the support is not focused on the specific needs of language learners largely due to the lack of expertise in the subject area by the special educator. But, this lack of language expertise on the part of the special educator is rarely acknowledged. Rather, the child's disability is blamed as the source of poor performance in the foreign language class.

Parental expectations for early language learning programs

Throughout our research, we have consistently found a linkage between parental support for foreign language in the elementary grades and student attitude and achievement. Other studies in the past have also posited that parents play a critical role in how children orient themselves to the introduction of a foreign language in the elementary school curriculum (Padilla & Sung, 1995; Rosenbusch, 1991; Met, 1998) and the influence of negative attitudes about language study that are transmitted to children in the home (Gardner, 1985). One of our studies (Donato et al., 1996) conducted during the third year of the Japanese program provides evidence that parents are not neutral in their attitudes about early language learning programs and have well-formed opinions and rank-ordered priorities concerning program goals and outcomes (see Chapter 5).

When asked to comment and reflect on her year of teaching in the Japanese program, the teacher corroborated the important role of these parents in the ambiance of her class. Two important parental involvement strategies were in place at the time – an evening Japanese class for parents that was eventually cancelled, and interactive homework assignments intended to connect parents to their children's learning of Japanese (Antonek et al., 1995). The teacher noted that one child seemed to lose interest in Japanese when she learned that the parents' evening Japanese class was cancelled. The teacher felt strongly that parents exerted an external influence because of their involvement with their children's learning and she seemed a bit discouraged with parents who refused to help their children on the interactive homework assignment. In cases of parental non-involvement, she observed a lack of motivation on the part of these students and a disinterest in learning Japanese.

Based on our work, we believe that the influence of the home attitude toward language learning is among the important factors that support or inhibit the growth of early foreign language programs. As such, parental influences and home-school linkages deserve serious consideration when determining the sustainability of innovative language programs. The types of behavioral commitments that parents make in the home, their expressed attitudes in the presence of their children toward other languages and cultures, and their opinions of program outcomes potentially shape children's involvement in language learning in the classroom. What remains puzzling is why these parents did not object more strongly to the closing of the Japanese program during the elementary school review process. Perhaps the *ad hoc* arrangement for the study of Japanese in the middle school and the lack of adequate yearly progress in foreign language led these parents to conclude that the program's contribution was not substantive enough to warrant its continuation.

Another fruitful line of inquiry to be added to this perspective is to understand how children perceive their home-school connections. In a series of unpublished studies conducted in New Zealand, Kaur found that children were aware of and indeed affected by their school's attempt to involve parents in their education. In some cases, children promoted connections between home and school for their own interests. In other cases, children actively worked against home-school relationships because of fear or embarrassment of the information that could be brought to light. When attempting to understand how parental influences affect the life and sustainability of early foreign language programs, both sides of the home-school relationship need to be examined. Studies have clearly shown the negative effects of parental attitude on children's achievement. Ultimately, however, the effects of parental attitude on a child's achievement rest largely on how the child perceives parental involvement in school life. In our studies, the children seem to have been affected by a lack of support that they perceived on the part of their parents or by the school's cancellation of the parent Japanese class. What we do not know is the role of the children in shaping these relationships in the home through their willingness or reluctance to talk about language learning with their parents. Research on the reciprocal contribution of child and parent attitudes and opinions on achievement and program credibility needs to be more carefully documented.

Pressure from other foreign language teachers

In both schools, we observed a similar phenomenon when early language learning programs were introduced. It is probably not an exaggeration to state that, for the teachers of languages other than that of the elementary program, the presence of an extended sequence in one foreign language created insecurities and uncertainties about the future of their own programs. As German and French teachers watched the K-8 Spanish program grow and take root in the school curriculum, they voiced concerns that their high school programs would be placed in jeopardy or that the school would eventually opt for a K-12 program offering only one foreign language, Spanish. At times, these fears led to anxiety over possible changes in their own programs and practices to accommodate potentially fewer students or a reduced number of classes. In the worst case, anxiety was aroused due to fear of losing one's position.

Another potentially damaging situation that might affect the sustainability of K-8 foreign language programs is unhealthy competition among languages. Unaware that a two-language option might be the positive outcome of the early introduction of foreign language learning, teachers can explicitly or implicitly promote the relative advantages of one language over another. Teachers' misconceived statements casually addressed to students such as, 'you can learn Spanish more quickly than Japanese', 'Spanish is a more useful language' or 'students make little progress in a foreign language in the elementary grades', can undermine programs and produce confusion in students concerning how languages are learned, the choice of language or the time when language learning should begin.

A final threat to the credibility and sustainability of early foreign language learners brought about unintentionally by other foreign language teachers is the misconception that the learning of one language will interfere or prevent the learning of another. In the early planning stages of the Spanish program, strong objections were raised by the chair of the foreign language department concerning the harmful effects of Spanish on the learning of French, in particular on French pronunciation. To help the teachers realize that learning two languages was possible and that students could acquire different foreign languages after the early introduction of Spanish, we recorded speech samples of students for analysis. The speech samples contained sentences read by students who were learning two languages simultaneously and students who were single language learners. The teachers were then asked to decide whether the student was a single or dual language learner based on their assessment of the students' pronunciation. It became clear that it was impossible to differentiate the two types of learners based on pronunciation in any systematic and reliable way beyond chance and guessing. This demonstration alleviated fears that early language learners would be disadvantaged if they opted to add a second foreign language to their academic program. Further, our research has also shown that knowing one foreign language has many positive effects on how students approach the learning of an additional language in terms of quantity of language learned and the quality of their learning (Sapienza et al., 2007).

In the case of the elementary school Spanish program, the initial fears of the elimination of the high school program in German and French were indeed unfounded. As the program matured and the students entered high school, no teaching position was lost, no classes were canceled or reduced, and French and German continued to thrive. Concerning the deleterious effects of learning one language on the learning of another, teachers experienced the opposite scenario. What was viewed anecdotally as a possible complication and obstacle to learning, in reality, has been proven false. Currently, German and French teachers are enthusiastic about their dual language learners. They state that they come to the language classroom with well-developed language learning strategies, more fully developed auditory memories and a greater tolerance for target language use in the classroom.

Summary

In this section, we have identified a variety of external and internal factors that affect the sustainability of foreign language programs. The demands of high-stakes testing in English language reading and mathematics have posed serious constraints on the time allotted for foreign language study. In many schools, time has been taken away from foreign language instruction to increase time devoted to subject areas for which a school's instructional performance is held legally accountable. In these situations, foreign language instruction is perceived to be not as important as other subjects and can be easily sacrificed. Although no 'hard data' exist at this time, M. Abbot, director of education for ACTFL has reported to us that elementary school programs nationally are being drastically reduced or eliminated because of the demands of NCLB. Clearly, this response to what needs to be done to modify time of instruction for other subject areas is telling, concerning the administrators' consciousness of, and commitment to, foreign language study in their school districts.

Parents of children with learning disabilities are often unsupportive of a program of study that includes what they perceive to be extraneous and unnecessary academic content. Unaware that a learning disability does not categorically exclude children from foreign language classes and that, in many cases, foreign language classes can be a source of success for children with learning disabilities, parents can be quite vocal and insistent that their children be removed from a program that has been regularized in the curriculum and intended for all students. Clearly, more research is needed to determine to what extent learning disabilities of particular kinds affect foreign language learning in children and in what ways, either positively or negatively. The voices of supportive parents of children with learning disabilities also need to be heard. Many teachers report that the vocal minority of parents who hold negative views of foreign language study for their children with disabilities often overpower the opinions of parents who see in the home the positive effects of language instruction in their children. These parental voices need to be documented systematically and their stories examined closely. Finally, the child who has an IEP can also often provide an important perspective on the issue, which is as valid and important to know as those of parents, teachers and special educators.

Another internal factor affecting children with learning disabilities in foreign language classes is that special educators are often unaware of current research and practice in foreign language learning and are poorly equipped to provide or suggest accommodations to foreign language teachers. When special education support teachers are included in the foreign language class, they often do not know the target language and their role is all too often reduced to clerical classroom responsibilities.

Parents and their expectations, possibly formed by their own previous language learning experiences, can also affect the sustainability of a program, the nature of program goals and the time allotted to language study. Where foreign language proficiency is not viewed as a goal and where the place of language study is seen as marginal to other subject areas, little parental support will be given for additional resources of time, materials and staff to build sustainable and substantive language programs.

Finally, teachers of other foreign languages who do not teach the language of the elementary school program can present obstacles to the health and credibility of programs. A failure to understand the cumulative benefits of early language learning programs on student interest in continued language study of other languages and on their language learning abilities in general, can create a school climate where language classes compete with each other through the promotion of studying one language over others. In the Spanish program, we watched the foreign language teachers' initial skepticism, fear and distrust of early language learning programs evolve into enthusiastic support when these students entered 'second foreign language classes' and teachers could experience first-hand what language learning at an early age means to future language study in high school.

In this chapter, we have reviewed from two perspectives the threats that we identified to sustaining elementary school language programs. In the following chapters, we will focus on how these issues that pose challenges to program sustainability were addressed by the two schools that we worked in and how they need to be seriously considered when implementing early foreign language programs.

Chapter 7
Emergent Themes of Successful Programs

The goal in this chapter is to identify, and then to describe, salient contrasting themes or characteristics of the two programs with which we worked with a view toward understanding why one of the programs ended abruptly and the other continues to thrive. The intention here is not to favor one program over another. It is hardly likely that either program had a clear understanding of the nature and requirements of educational sustainability when they set out to introduce their respective curricular innovations. Our purpose here is to analyze and identify, based on our work in these schools, the features that might account for the longevity of one program in contrast to the termination of the other. Moreover, as we will present in the next chapter, the Japanese program that ended in 2005 was replaced in 2006 by a K-8 Spanish program that was developed and implemented following the model of the Spanish program about which we have reported in previous chapters. In other words, the school did not lose its interest in foreign language in the elementary grades, but rather replaced Japanese with Spanish for reasons we will discuss later.

In the subsequent sections, we examine the following characteristics that emerged in one school district that has developed a successful and sustainable K-12 foreign language program: (a) the vision for the program, (b) support for the teachers and attention to curricular issues across grade levels, (c) concern for participating students and (d) the positioning of the program within the life of the school and total school curriculum.

The *Vision* for the Program

We have come to conclude that the *vision* for the program must resonate positively among all the varied stakeholders for the program to be sustainable. The vision must be shared, endorsed and regularly revisited. The vision that inspired the implementation of the Japanese program was essentially one that was imposed from a decision that was made by the school board. The underlying rationale – to introduce students to the study of an important Asian language and culture at a time (the early 1990s) when much attention was focused on East Asia – was certainly a commendable one. However, the decision to begin a Japanese program was essentially imposed on the school and made in the absence of input from the various constituents and recipients of the program. There were no prior discussions with parents or teachers, hence the program never really became one of the defining attributes of the school that offered the Japanese program, although this was the initial intention of the board when it decided to introduce this unique curricular offering. This observation is not meant to denigrate the board's decision or mode of implementation. Indeed, the board comprised a committed group continually working to improve the school's visibility, to expand the school's academic offerings and to situate the school among those unique school districts that, at the time, opted to offer a less commonly taught language to its students. In many ways, at the time, the board was placed in the unenviable position of trying to improve a school that was already held in high regard by many.

In the school district offering Spanish, on the other hand, the superintendent wanted a foreign language program for the school district 'because of a sense that American education was behind [the rest of the world] with regard to exposure to foreign languages'. In Tucker *et al.* (2001), we provide a detailed description of the development and implementation of this program, including interviews with parents, teachers, administrators and board members. Comments and opinions of school district constituents in this section are taken directly from this study.

From the time that the school district's superintendent first proposed the idea of a foreign language program beginning at the elementary level as part of the district's plans for consolidating several community schools in one new facility, his vision was widely discussed and resonated positively throughout the group of administrators, teachers and school board members. This widespread acceptance was largely due to the superintendent's self-proclaimed commitment to foreign language education and to the preparation of graduates for the demands of working in a world where globalization had become the norm. His commitment was perceived by all and his vision of a school district where students would graduate with foreign language proficiency was embraced as a worthwhile goal at a time when school consolidation and curricular revision was paramount.

The ultimate selection of Spanish as the language to be taught was not particularly important, although the community was polled by means of a questionnaire concerning the choice of language and Spanish surfaced as the majority's choice. However, during interviews, we learned that most respondents 'felt strongly that a foreign language should be introduced, but it didn't matter [to them] which one'. Clearly, this response corroborated our observation that the superintendent's vision was shared by the wider community in the school district.

Representatives from the administration, teachers, community members and parents all agreed that for their students to be viable citizens prepared to participate in the global knowledge economy of the 21st century, '[they] needed knowledge of another language'. Their students should be prepared to compete for jobs in a global market, where other students would have the benefit of school systems that emphasized the learning of several languages. Students who were interviewed expressed dissatisfaction with the status quo; after several years of foreign language instruction in French, German or Spanish at the secondary school level, many often could remember no more than a few key phrases. Many of the adult respondents also echoed this frustration with regard to their own language experience in school.

In addition, respondents reported that a foreign language program would help elevate the reputation of the school district. As one respondent pointed out, 'This definitely seemed a way of making them better, and improving their reputation as a leadership district... It was also a way to show the people that this was something they could do for the children, to improve cultural awareness, and improve their self esteem as well'. Not only would the establishment of an early foreign language program show their willingness to try innovative new programs, but it would also demonstrate their dedication to doing things that would benefit the students.

All respondents to the survey that we conducted reported that the success of the program was due in large part to the careful planning that went into the development and implementation of the program. The most crucial part of this planning revolved around the involvement of all the stakeholders: the members of the school board and the administrators, of course; but also the teachers, the parents, student representatives, community members and university partners. All stakeholders were continually encouraged to 'raise their concerns so that they could be addressed, instead of complaining in isolation later'. As one administrator pointed out, 'This one was done right. Sometimes when school districts make a decision to implement a program, they're not always careful to get all of the stakeholders to buy in'.

The concept of 'empowerment' was also central to many of the interviews. Respondents were unanimous that they felt 'ownership' of the foreign language program from the beginning. This sense of ownership contrasted sharply with the Japanese school where decisions were made behind closed doors among a select group of individuals who were not expected to engage in collaborative decision making. The early discussions surrounding the implementation of the Spanish program were seen as drawing on 'the philosophy of teamwork in the district'. Respondents reported that they were 'never hesitant to voice a very small concern because... you know any comments are treated with respect and addressed'. This empowerment that teachers, department heads, principals and others felt was clearly the result of the strong leadership provided by the superintendent who saw his position as one that would 'allow him to guide "the powers that be" toward the inclusion of the program [centrally within the core curriculum for the district]'.

For the Spanish program that has survived, and indeed flourished, a shared vision resonated with all stakeholders. For the Japanese program that was terminated, we find an externally imposed vision that was never fully embraced by any of the potential stakeholders. In this case, although the program continued for several years, the effects of the initial development and implementation process was never neutralized and ultimately led to the demise of the program in 2005.

Support for the Teachers

The administrators are not, of course, the ones charged with the daily implementation, operation and care of the program. That responsibility falls inevitably to the language teachers. Here, too, an enormous difference in terms of the moral and practical support that was provided for the Japanese teachers and for the Spanish teachers was found.

A theme that contributes to the overall effectiveness of a foreign language program is the *quality* of its foreign language faculty. At the primary and intermediate grades (K-5), the Spanish program has placed a strong priority on hiring teachers who are certified in both foreign language education *and* elementary education. As history has taught us, teachers who import approaches and methods of foreign language instruction from the upper grades into the elementary school usually do not provide the type of instruction appropriate to the learner. However, teachers who understand how children learn, regularly prepare and teach age-appropriate lessons that take into account the capacity and natural curiosity for language learning that young children bring to the classroom. The teachers of the Japanese program, on the other hand, although excellent – indeed one of them was truly charismatic – did not share this type of preparation.

The notion of support for the teachers took many forms. In the school implementing the Spanish program, for example, a good deal of attention was paid to ensuring that the Spanish program was incorporated into the regular curriculum of the primary, intermediate and then middle school with a minimum of disruption. Care was taken to assist the Spanish teachers through continuing linkage with the grade-appropriate teachers and with the university partners, and by the systematic provision of discussion and in-service training through their participation in the monthly meetings of the Foreign Language Steering Committee. The Spanish curriculum was not developed in isolation from the rest of the elementary school curriculum. Rather, Spanish was added to the curriculum framework that was driven by essential questions treated across a variety of subject areas, now to include Spanish. From the beginning, the approach to curriculum planning anchored Spanish in the total school curriculum. Through its position in the curriculum, Spanish was perceived as an equally important subject supporting the academic goals of the elementary school.

Respondents to our survey noted that the Spanish teachers 'had the support of the classroom teachers; they've really accepted it, they're learning the language and speaking it with their students, and they reinforce what they're learning [in Spanish] all throughout the day'. The principal of the primary school noted that he devotes a good deal of attention to ensuring that the regular classroom teachers are 'attempting to implement the Spanish instruction in their daily lessons as well'. For the most part, this pattern of welcoming and acceptance never developed in the Japanese program. The program's various teachers over the years were essentially 'isolates' who developed their lesson plans and taught their classes without any systematic opportunity to incorporate their work into the fabric or the life of the school.

This lack of connection to the broader school curriculum was also revealed in the reflections of the teacher in year 2 of the program, who expressed some concern over the program's lack of integration into the wider school community and her own personal feeling of marginalization from the overall academic and social life of the school. The feeling of marginalization seemed to persist in her relationship to other teachers and in her understanding of the place of Japanese in the total

K-5 curriculum. She claimed she knew homeroom teachers better in year 2, but that their relationship to her did not change much from the first year of the program. She admitted that this may have been due to scheduling difficulties and the inability to find an appropriate time to meet and discuss their classes and how they could be connected to Japanese lessons. She stated that the Japanese program 'is a little bit isolated from the main program', and she wondered how seriously it was taken by the school, parents and other teachers.

At the same time, lest our analysis be perceived as being unfairly negative, we want to note that the Japanese teachers have all been concerned for the academic and personal well being of their students. They have all been what we would describe as truly reflective practitioners who make instructional decisions and modifications based on classroom observation and evidence. They have shared their plans and their practices with one another and with members of the profession more broadly through participation in annual meetings of associations such as the Northeast Conference on the Teaching of Foreign Languages (NEC) and the Pennsylvania State Modern Language Association (PSMLA). They have attended research meetings, provided detailed feedback on their teaching experiences, provided written communiqués in journals and have developed and modified the curriculum based on observations of their students' performance and their own classroom practice.

Nonetheless, we are left to conclude that the Japanese teacher's lack of substantive and productive interactions with other teachers around the topic of curriculum was one of the major factors that led to the marginalization of the program and to its ultimate demise.

Concern for Participating Students

An overriding concern of the teachers and the Spanish program's steering committee has been that students make continual progress in their foreign language proficiency. All stakeholders share a common goal – as students progress in the program, they are expected to progress in their linguistic and cultural knowledge. Proficiency outcomes are critical to the success and sustainability of foreign language programs since observations of early language learning programs across the country often reveal that children are faced with repetition of the same content presented in the same way from one year to the next (see Donato *et al.*, 2000 for evidence for this assertion and for possible explanations).

The Japanese program was characterized by a repetitive curriculum that, owing to the full implementation of the program (K-5) in one year, was not able to develop, gradually and sequentially, the scope of instruction across the years. This inability to attend to articulation issues happened for a number of reasons – perhaps the most critical was that there were many newcomers each year to the program across the various grades and there was no provision for providing supplementary instruction to newcomers. So the teacher was effectively forced to 'start again' each year. As new students entered the program at various grade levels, the Japanese teachers faced the challenge of simultaneously expanding the language ability and cultural understandings of continuing students while bringing new students to a level of ability that would allow them to participate fully and make progress in cohort classes. Clearly, a full implementation model is complex and hard to manage especially when the responsibility for the curriculum is in the hands of one teacher.

In the Spanish program, on the other hand, a summer program for newcomers was instituted in the school district, which offered an introduction to the Spanish language and cultures. In this short program, newcomers were taught rudimentary lessons that provided background in Spanish to allow these students to participate in classes without feeling left behind or incapable of contributing to the class. Additionally, a system of 'buddies' (i.e. the *Amigos* program) paired each newcomer with a veteran of the program who could provide tutorial guidance and assistance both within and outside class. Lastly, the Spanish program maintains a telephone 'hotline' where students (or their parents) can call for assistance on homework assignments or information on the lessons of the week. Conversely, the one school-home linkage mediated through the interactive homework program for parents of the Japanese students was discontinued after a successful three-year period (Antonek *et al.*, 1995).

This concern for participating students and the sustained assistance that has been provided to enhance the likelihood of their successful participation in classes clearly differentiated the two programs. We argue that teacher support for the thorny issue of newcomers to a foreign language program was an important element in the long-term sustainability of the Spanish program. By extension, the complexity of the Japanese program, namely, a single specialist teacher who was faced with the difficult task of refining four to five grade levels of curriculum each year while simultaneously addressing the demands of newcomers integrated into intact classes, led to a lack of curricular articulation necessary for ensuring progress for all students. As we have learned, where student progress in language and culture is not visible and measurable, confidence in the program and its value will soon falter.

Positioning the Program within the Life of the School

Despite the fact that the Japanese program persisted for more than a decade, it clearly remained a marginal program with questionable results concerning student learning. Over the years, the Japanese classes were always among the first to be sacrificed when additional time was needed to rehearse for a spring play or musical production or when the students attended a field trip. Except for one brief period during the winter of 1998 when the Nagano Olympic Games were in session, the program never became a defining feature for the school. Japanese classes never enjoyed the same scheduling privileges as other subject areas and were inserted, at times, during breaks from core subject classes, such as mathematics. As one elementary school student noted during an interview, 'Japanese class is like a commercial during our regular classes'. As this student clearly perceived, learning Japanese was not on equal footing with other subjects and demanded less attention and seriousness than other subjects.

Conversely, the Spanish program has been central to the school district from its initiation to the district's continuing strategic plan for the future. The curriculum was developed following the school-district template for planned courses of study in all subject areas. That is, each thematically organized unit was specified according to (1) student learning outcomes; (2) content, materials and activities; and (3) procedures for assessment. During curriculum planning, every attempt was made to integrate Spanish with ongoing activities in art, music, library, physical education and the computer curriculum. Additionally, during our interviews with various stakeholders, several concerns related to the future of foreign language learning in the district were brought sharply into focus. The most resounding theme reflected the realization that issues of articulation and integration would be critical if the district were to have a coherent, viable and sustainable foreign language program across 13 years of instruction. Although not a new topic to the foreign language education field, we have learned that articulation and integration is more than just good standards-based curriculum planning practice. It is the key to ensuring sustainable and credible foreign language programs in school districts.

Over the years since the program's inception in 1996–1997, we have consistently seen instances of collaborative program and curricular planning. The planning involved school principals, language teachers, academic content teachers and university partners working hand in hand to ensure that the curricula had been well articulated and that there was the clearest possible integration of language and content goals – particularly as the program moved in to the middle school years of grades 6–8. The Spanish program has clearly been incorporated into the life of the school district in ways that simply never happened with the Japanese program. By means of linking Spanish to the curriculum of the elementary school and implementing content-based instruction in the middle school, two visible and concrete means of integration made possible the endorsement of the Spanish program by the district and defined it as an important and valuable component of the district's goals. As the director of instruction, stated, 'one of the strategies used in the school district was to establish foreign language as an integral part of the core curriculum and to use an approach of integrated content-based instruction... Rather than taking away from other curricular areas, the FL program reinforces and gives students additional instructional opportunities for developing broad skills and knowledge' (Gori, 2002: 614).

It is also noteworthy that ongoing research into a foreign language program may also be a key factor in positioning a program's importance in the district. How research on the program is positioned in the school district is as important as the positioning of the program itself. In both schools, we have been able to conduct end-of-year assessments across grade levels to track student progress and classroom-based studies to understand the day-to-day instruction and its potential impact on student performance. We have examined classroom discursive interactions between teachers and students, analyzed different teachers presenting the same content-based lessons and documented student participation and perceptions during classroom instruction. In both schools, we have closely analyzed writing samples to determine students' growth in literacy across various textual genres. In all cases, our goal was to monitor and document student achievement in terms of grade-level articulation and student outcomes. In addition, our research sought to understand the successes and challenges of implementing serious foreign language study across the grades in an already crowded curriculum.

What is intriguing and perhaps relevant to ensuring sustainable foreign language programs in elementary schools is the reception of research efforts. Although both schools were sites of ongoing yearly research into various programmatic features, only in one case were the results of research used as feedback to the program for instructional and curriculum modifications. In the case of the Spanish program, meetings at the opening of the school year included reports of the previous year's testing and grade-level comparisons of student progress. These reports were delivered by the teachers who played an active role in end-of-year assessment development and in oral interviews and scoring and subsequent curricular revisions based on research findings. For example, in year 7 of the program, elementary school students were found to outperform middle school students on written assessments. This finding was a cause of concern for the teachers particularly because the middle school program was content-based and required literacy skills to explore and learn academic content in a foreign language. Based on this finding, middle schools teachers reviewed their curriculum and significantly expanded literacy opportunities for students. Elementary school Spanish teachers, pleased by their students' performance, continued to focus on reading and writing, knowing how these skills would be necessary when their students entered the middle school program. In short, the reception of research was welcoming, open to change and new ideas, and exciting, as teachers saw evidence of their efforts and areas that needed attention.

By contrast, research into Japanese never took root in the life of the school in the same way as it was used in the Spanish program. Journal articles were published and professional presentations and end-of-year reports were produced. However, the products of research remained largely within our research group and results were never broadly disseminated in the local community.

Many reasons may account for why this difference was noted. First, the lack of collaborative planning and evaluation by a steering committee and a single member foreign language faculty may not have provided a strong enough model of a collaborative culture of change (Fullan, 2000) for publicly and jointly reflecting on research results. In short, the Japanese program had no audience, beside the teacher, to receive the research news. Second, as we have established before, the Japanese program never became a fully functioning part of the school's curriculum and never matured beyond a 'special subject' and unique feature of the school. For serious deliberation about research findings to occur, a foreign language program must abandon its uniqueness status and be regarded with the same expectations of performance and the same need for evaluation as other subject areas. In short, research was not on the minds of the program constituents since the expectations of a special program differed from that of core curricular subjects. The goals of the Japanese program were simply not on equal footing with other classes. This lack of curricular equity was due perhaps to a misinformed assumption about what children can actually achieve in elementary school foreign language programs. Given this scenario, it is not surprising that research was not expected and embraced by the school and, thus, played no role in making concrete changes to the program. Perhaps the lesson to be learned is that foreign language education needs to be in the hands of foreign language educators and not in the hands of those who may seek to begin programs for reasons other than those stated in the National Standards for Foreign Language Learning goals of foreign language education. Initiating a program based on language popularity, the provision of federal monies for strategic languages or an attempt to make the school unique in some way may indeed result in a foreign language program. Whether these initiatives and the motivations that they engender create sustainable programs is dubious.

Summary

The profile that has emerged from our work over the years provides, we believe, important lessons for others who may embark on similar foreign language grade-level expansions and curricular innovations. Our longitudinal research has enabled us to identify and examine, in actual practice, the key characteristics for developing and implementing a well articulated and apparently successful foreign language program. We fully believe that the school district's lived experience with the implementation of a sustainable Spanish foreign language program is one that is both generalizable and replicable to other settings.

The direction and decisions of this district rested on the concerns of several important constituents and reflects Markee's (1997) observation that innovative projects are affected, positively or negatively, by complex sociocultural variables, such as cultural beliefs, political climate, historical and economic conditions, administrative attitudes, institutional support, and technological, sociolinguistic and language planning factors (see also Holliday, 1994). When viewed globally these themes – *vision, support, concern* and *positioning* – refract and reflect all the sociocultural variables identified by Markee and attest to their importance, as well as the need to acknowledge and address openly these factors when designing and implementing new programs that we hope will be sustainable.

In the next chapter, we link the concept of language program sustainability and the key features that we have identified within the framework of economic, social and environmental sustainable development. We will argue that the concepts of sustainable material development may also be applied to the development of sustainable intellectual development within school districts. That is, sustainable foreign language educational development requires carefully planning resource allocation to meet the foreign language education needs of our students while simultaneously preserving current positive educational practices and ensuring that these foreign language needs can be met in the indefinite future.

Chapter 8
Summary and Conclusions

In the following sections, we discuss program sustainability from the perspective of the lessons that we have learned through our research with the Japanese and Spanish programs. These 'lessons' include the importance of continually ensuring growth in language proficiency and cultural understanding. We will also discuss the importance of factors internal and external to the program, namely, the anchoring of the program into the school, constituent collaboration and school district-university partnerships. We will then present the implications that we see for other districts that may be contemplating launching a new program or expanding an existing program and the need for them to take into account factors to ensure sustainable programs through the years. Finally, we discuss the implications that we see for future research. From these three perspectives, we generalize a model of sustainable foreign language program development with reference to the features of sustainable economic, social and environmental development. We provide an example of our model of sustainable program development through a discussion of two schools – one that was not successful at sustaining their Japanese program and one that created a Spanish program that has continued for many years. We also show how the Japanese school recovered from the elimination of K-5 foreign language education program and re-instated, from our perspective, a sustainable Spanish program based on the principles of sustainable development that we have presented.

Lessons We Have Learned

We have learned three major lessons in our work over the years, and we turn now to a brief presentation and discussion of each of these.

How to ensure steady growth in language proficiency

We have learned over the years that a necessary component of sustainable program development is visible and concrete signs of gains in language proficiency. Programs cannot hope to be recommended for continuation if parents, administrators and other teachers perceive a lack of student progress during the time allotted for this instruction, time that is often taken away from other subject areas. From this perspective, the program must be viewed by the larger social structure of the school as worth the time, effort and expense. In our work in the Japanese program, we often heard parents lament the lack of growth in proficiency that they observed in their children. We also noted that the children expressed boredom and frustration in their comments when they experienced what they perceived to be repetitive and recycled lessons each year. As we have indicated, the conditions of the Japanese program were largely responsible for this lack of progress. The fact that the program depended on a sole itinerant teacher who was responsible for all levels of instruction from the beginning made careful curricular articulation impossible and overwhelming. By contrast, the Spanish program produced results from the beginning and, because of the value placed on the children's learning, received strong community support.

To ensure visible growth in proficiency, we have learned that several programmatic procedures need to be firmly in place. First, those who are unaware of how languages are taught and learned should not be in decision-making positions when developing and implementing elementary school foreign language programs. Steering committees and *ad hoc* planning groups need to recruit the expertise of language educators to learn about curricular articulation and its importance to ensure steady growth in proficiency. This also implies that the subject area must be perceived as serious and that all should understand that instruction in a foreign language can produce academic gains. If members of planning committees view a foreign language program as only enrichment, exploration or a unique feature of the school and do not situate the foreign language program among the other academic subjects, the result will be the inevitable criticism of the program as, bluntly put, a waste of time. The irony of this reaction by constituents is that often the conditions under which the language program operates preclude any possibility of growth in language learning. Where proficiency is not a goal, student language gains will be impossible to realize. Moreover, the source of this instructional discontinuity in language study can be traced to the lack of clearly articulated shared goals and outcomes for language learning in a seamless sequence of instruction.

A second way to ensure growth in proficiency, assuming that proficiency constitutes an agreed upon conscious goal of the program, is to assess program outcomes yearly and systematically. The assessment of the cumulative effects of the program on student proficiency requires careful planning of curriculum-based assessments of all modes of communication and requires the active participation of teachers in the process of test development. Results of yearly assessments need to be reviewed by the faculty and others in decision-making positions concerning the future of the program. Summaries of assessments need to be written and disseminated and curricular revisions need to take place based on assessment results. As we have discussed previously, the Spanish program included active and systematic assessment of student progress each year and teachers were empowered to interpret test results and make decisions concerning areas for improvements. The Dominquez study (2003a, 2003b) and her work with teachers is a clear example of using program assessment to contribute directly to program improvements that were found to be consequential for student progress across all grade levels in the later years of our study.

Curricular diversification is also necessary to maintain student interest and engagement in learning the new language. Wudthayagorn (2000) discovered that there were noticeable drops in motivation as students moved through the grades, particularly in the middle school. This dip in motivation, however, is not impossible to reverse. Chinen et al. (2003) discovered that the introduction of a new procedure in the middle school Japanese program, that is, the use of a portfolio assessment procedure, created conditions of increased motivation among children who had previously expressed disinterest and a lack of motivation for continuing their study of Japanese. Simply having extended sequences of instruction does not ensure that students will grow in proficiency. Based on our experiences, we believe the real issue is what students are learning and doing in these years of instruction and how instruction in one year builds on what students know and can do from previous years. A continual challenge for teachers in early language learning programs has been establishing developmentally appropriate instruction for children as they mature socially, emotionally and academically in the context of programs that are often established in less than ideal conditions and, sometimes, for less than ideal reasons. We cannot hope for gains in proficiency without conscious attention to diversifying instructional practices across time to meet the development levels of students in the elementary school.

The importance of collaboration among constituents

As we have discussed earlier, the social conditions in which foreign language programs are planned and implemented are consequential to ensuring the permanence of program health, growth and credibility.

The success of the Spanish program can be traced, in large part, to the consciously planned involvement of individuals who were not directly associated with the everyday operations of the program. This planning contrasted sharply with the Japanese program where decisions were made largely outside the societal circle in which the program was located.

We have learned that the opinions of constituents matter. Constituents are those who are loosely linked to the program, but not responsible for its day-to-day operations, such as parents, other subject area teachers and school board members. Although they may be viewed as not central to the program, their role in promoting and sustaining new programs is not to be underestimated. If the time comes for program reduction or elimination, these individuals may be the very ones to express dissatisfaction with programmatic revisions. Without their support, programs can disappear very easily with much less effort than it took to implement the foreign language instruction at the onset. Recruiting their input and support is necessary for programs to flourish and survive. Care was taken in the Spanish program to include in the decision-making process the opinions and attitudes of the school-based constituents and the wider community in which the district was located when first planning the elementary school program. The superintendent formed a Foreign Language Program Committee to oversee the planning and implementation of a new and innovative foreign language program. Committee members consisted of the district's director of curriculum who chaired the group, the superintendent, principals from the primary, intermediate and middle schools, selected teachers, the chair of the secondary school foreign languages department and the university collaborators. The committee began its work by conducting a community survey that led to the selection of Spanish as the foreign language to be taught. The committee also carefully planned for implementing the program year by year beginning with kindergarten in 1996–1997 and adding a grade level per year (see Tucker & Donato, 2003, for a description of the planning and implementation process). The work of the committee is particularly relevant to acquisition planning and demonstrates the value of micro-level language planning activities embedded in immediate and interconnected academic and local communities.

By contrast, the Japanese program was decided on in isolation from those who would participate indirectly in the program. The school board decided on the choice of language of instruction and the community's reactions to the selection of Japanese was not solicited. Only after our initial parent survey at the end of the first year of the program did we realize the strong objection that some parents expressed toward the teaching of Japanese over, e.g. German or Spanish. What this reaction revealed to us is that programs cannot be developed in isolation from the social context in which they operate. Most importantly, constituents' opinions need to be expressed and taken into consideration when developing programs. When the time had come for the Japanese program to close because of the departure of the teacher, few, if any, parents spoke against this decision. This silence indicated a tacit acceptance of the program's closure and dramatically illustrated the lack of support that these parents felt toward the teaching of Japanese in the elementary grades. The exceptional cases aside, for a program to be sustained, broad-based support is needed. Creating this support can come about by sharing information on planning, soliciting suggestions about the language of study and program models, and widely disseminating the vision for the program, information about student achievement and plans for the future. The support of parents and other teachers in the school can be powerful forces in preserving language education in the elementary grades and can be created simply by including them in the planning process and informing them regularly about the achievements of the programs.

The benefits of a school district-university partnership

A third feature of sustainability involves partnership between university foreign language educators and school districts. Although both schools received the benefits of a school-university partnership, only in the case of the Spanish program was the partnership valued as critical to the success of the program. One reason that this partnership was actively recruited and perceived as necessary and important may have been the vision and complexity of the Spanish program compared to the single-teacher program model in the case of Japanese. Several grade level teachers, clear proficiency goals and a vision of a K-12 program where content-based instruction would be the model for the middle and high school presented unique curricular and scheduling challenges and led to a perceived need for the knowledge of those inside the field with experience in elementary school language program design.

Three features characterize a productive school district-university partnership. First, a climate of sharing resources is necessary where diverse knowledge, skills and background are pooled during program design, implementation and evaluation. What was striking about the

Spanish program was the intense level of involvement of school principals, administrative personnel and subject area teachers in the core decisions for the program. For example, during the early planning of end-of-year assessments, the then-principal of the intermediate school (grades 3–5), who was an art teacher, contributed significantly to the design of oral assessment. Based on her knowledge of integrative language arts and art teaching, she proposed a model for eliciting student language based on drawings that the students created in their art classes. Her suggestion was implemented with success and the challenge of creating the conditions for eliciting target language talk from young learners in a low-stress interview format was alleviated. The point here is that sharing resources should not be limited only to those who deem themselves language teaching specialists. In elementary schools, many individuals have deep knowledge of children and how they learn, which is often lacking in the preparation of a foreign language teacher who does not specialize in one level of instruction and must be a K-12 foreign language generalist. Recruiting the diverse knowledge and skills of those who are directly connected to the education of elementary school children can yield important insights, solutions and new directions.

Second, shared leadership in the form of collaborative decision making and problem solving are necessary components of productive partnerships. By distributing decision making and problem solving throughout the school, multiple perspectives on program issues and a wide range of possible solutions emerge. Program leadership derives, therefore, from the multiple perspectives of groups, the knowledge they co-construct, the anxieties they experience and manage, and the connections they forge while maintaining open-ended exploration (Fullan, 2000). For collaborations to be productive, university partners cannot position themselves as the authority and sole source of knowledge. Productive partnerships must see program leadership not within the traits and attributes of individuals or their assigned duties, but within the social web of an organization and the shared roles and responsibilities of all its members (Ogawa & Bossert, 2000). From this perspective, program leadership is a systemic quality not located in one person or another, but mapped through the collaborations of individuals within an entire organization. Whether it is a foreign language teacher, professor, curriculum supervisor, principal or superintendent, the new leadership team is able to weave various perspectives to construct the positive scenarios of action and fundamental change. In this way, neither the school district not the university partners become vulnerable to, and dependent on, external answers (Fullan, 2000) and create solutions that are superior to those of any single member of the collaboration.

Third, and related to the idea of shared leadership, is the need for a collaboratively constructed research program. In foreign language education, we typically seek knowledge of teaching by looking to a variety of authoritative accounts that we assume apply in practice. When we invoke research, it is often based on studies external to the unique context of teaching foreign languages in American schools. School districts often look to authorities outside their teaching context, and assume too easily that research actually has something to say about their local teaching and learning situations. Simply compiling what we know will be of no benefit if we cannot tease out what information applies and what information does not apply to whom. As Freeman (1998, 2000) points out, we often look for knowledge about language teaching and learning activity in all the wrong places. Even in the context of this book, not all of our experiences might apply to all programs. Even these recommendations need to be evaluated for their usefulness against the backdrop of local and school-based issues. One size simply does not fit all.

Collaborative partnerships can create knowledge of the program and the activity of teaching foreign language to young children, contribute to the school program and potentially inform the profession. According to Freeman (2000), the knowledge that animates language teaching and learning can and needs to be found within the *activity of teaching* itself. Moreover, this knowledge emanates from the collaborative inquiry into the specifics of teaching rather than the consumption and acceptance of the authoritative concepts of others. Knowledge of the activity of teaching includes, therefore, how teachers and students conduct their work together, the social context in which they teach and learn, the unspoken norms and stated rules of classroom life and the instructional tools they use to achieve curricular goals. This knowledge cannot be gained without sharing perspectives on the program and validating the local conditions in which the program is situated. Collaborative research on program dynamics and learning outcomes with teachers is one way to ensure creating locally important knowledge.

According to Fullan (2000), this type of research takes place through collaborative investigations and the sharing of day-to-day skills, knowledge and expertise. Discussing and sharing research possibilities is one powerful aspect of school district-university partnerships. Schools know that knowledge of teaching is located within teachers and their day-to-day practice. University researchers understand how to uncover teachers' tacit knowledge and transform it into useable information (Freeman, 1998, 2000) and how to establish assessments that produce comparable and useful information about the state of the program. From this perspective, research leadership in schools needs to be located in this collaboration and requires the insight of all participants in generating questions, developing investigations, and analyzing and interpreting findings. Research efforts brought about through school district-university partnerships ensure programs that renew themselves yearly by addressing areas of improvement identified in the collaboratively and locally constructed research efforts.

Implications for Other Districts

During our involvement with these two programs, now in the 16th year and continuing, we have learned two important lessons that we believe have implications for other districts – the importance of engaging in systematic 'acquisition planning' prior to implementation or major expansion, and the importance of drawing on local resources that are sure to be available.

Acquisition planning for the future

We draw on the construct of acquisition planning in the sense that the term has been used in the language education planning and policy literature by Cooper (1990) to refer to an active process undertaken by the local entity – an independent school, a school district, a state education agency or even a national ministry of education – to assess needs, to canvass prospective stakeholders and to implement a program that benefits from a shared consensus that there will be local support for the program. As we have described, the Japanese program was implemented in a 'top down' fashion without an initial survey (whether formal or informal) to 'test the waters' and without taking steps to engage prospective participants in the various stages of decision making. The result was the eventual elimination of the program – with little expressed unhappiness on the part of parents, students or teachers at the school.

The Spanish program, on the other hand, continues to thrive. The initial cohort of students is completing grade 11 as we write this monograph and a substantial proportion of them will continue to grade 12. The program is still a required, and regular, component of the district's curriculum for *all* students from kindergarten through grade 7 – despite the pressures being exerted on the district to demonstrate *adequate yearly progress* in reading, writing and mathematics. We believe that the sustainability of the program depends, in large measure, on the fact that the program belongs to a wide range of key stakeholders who had an active voice in the decision to introduce a language, in the choice of language and in the systematic planning for the articulated introduction of the program year by year.

We strongly urge other districts or agencies that are planning to introduce new programs or to significantly expand existing ones to test the waters beforehand, rather than later wishing that they had done so. We also want to convey the message that there are very probably resource people in the community who can be called on for various types of assistance.

Availability of professional assistance from multiple sources

Those of us who work in Schools of Education (Donato) or departments of Modern Languages (Tucker) or in numerous other university-based disciplines are, for the most part, eager to be involved in addressing school-based challenges of program development and implementation. We are able to assist in a variety of ways, ranging from the general sharing of so-called best practices with administrators and teachers, to the more hands on assistance with curriculum development, teacher training, test development and sharing of progress reports with various constituencies. The *quid pro quo* for such assistance is usually an agreement to provide access for the researchers' doctoral students to classes and planning meetings and to allow research teams to collect, analyze and report information about the programs and the progress of students in a variety of public scholarly forums. The researchers, for their part, of course agree to be governed by stringent ethical guidelines during their interaction with members of the school community and with the appropriate guarantees of anonymity and confidentiality.

Implications for Additional Research

We bring two quite different sets of experience to bear on our collaborative research. Donato is an applied linguist by training with extensive experience in classroom-based research and language teaching theory and practice. Tucker is an experimental psychologist by training with extensive experience in language policy and planning and language program evaluation. Both have an interest in helping to improve the quality of language education programs and to ensuring broader opportunities for participation. We are both aware that a plethora of myths continue to surround the discussions about whether, when and for how long to implement foreign language programs, and we both remain convinced that additional research with clear reporting of outcomes to policy makers and parents as well as to fellow researchers will be absolutely essential in the years ahead. We wish here to emphasize two priorities – the value of replication and the need for longitudinal research.

The value of replication

Over the years, we have tried to carry out our research in a series of interlocking steps so that we have the opportunity to observe and to collect information from cohorts of students not only when they comprise the lead group that is experiencing a new program or new intervention, but also to return a year or two or three later to collect information from a cohort that is participating in the program in its second or third year of implementation. For a variety of reasons, such as the so-called 'experimenter expectancy' or 'Pygmalion effect' (Rosenthal & Jacobson, 1992) or the fact that the second iteration of a new class offering often differs significantly from the first, we believe it useful to replicate data collection so that one observes and collects information, for example, from fifth grade Spanish students in 2002 and again from another cohort of fifth grade students in 2005 and 2008.

We find that replication enhances our confidence in the phenomena that we are observing, and that reports from replicated research also enhance the likelihood that a message will be positively received by diverse target audiences.

The need for longitudinal research

Unfortunately, there has been a paucity of longitudinal educational research of any kind over the years. This is true for a variety of reasons – the fickleness of funding agencies, the changing interests of researchers or even changes in school administrators and their levels of interest in questions from previous administrations. The classic study that is usually studied as an exemplary tracking study is that by Terman and associates at Stanford University (see, e.g. Terman, 1925; Terman & Olden, 1959). In general, the research showed that the 'gifted' or high IQ individuals that they followed over time, came to differ markedly from supposedly similar cohorts of individuals. Thus, the gifted group maintained and, on many dimensions, even increased their early superiority. Their incidence of ill health, mortality, insanity, delinquency and alcoholism was well below that of the general population of corresponding age. In addition, higher proportions of the gifted cohort entered college, graduated, earned honors and awards, and went on to post-graduate education, etc. The differences accentuated over time and the research methodology added to the value of collecting longitudinal data of this type, typically conducted within the medical and biological sciences but woefully absent in foreign language education classroom studies.

Unfortunately, there are very few extant longitudinal research studies in the language education field in areas that have informed both policy and practice. The only ones that come immediately to mind are the 12-year longitudinal evaluation of the effects of participation in French immersion programs by English-speaking youngsters (Lambert & Tucker, 1982), the tracking study of the cumulative effects on teachers of participating in an NDEA summer training institute (Bruck et al., 1975) and the 23-year study [to date] of early participation in high quality preschool programs (Schweinhart & Weikart, 1997). To make three complex stories very brief, over time the data revealed effects or patterns of development that would not have been predicted by a series of cross-sectional snapshots taken at any one point or even at multiple points in time. The results demonstrated to us that such longitudinal study is absolutely essential for documenting the cumulative benefits associated with any type of educational intervention. Many stories cannot be told accurately without the longitudinal perspective that permits the blossoming and nurturing of the so-called 'defining moment'.

The policy implications that derive from the results of longitudinal research can also be enormous. To take but one example, a program of French-immersion education that began in *one* school in *one* community in the Province of Quebec has, over time, spread to become a natural and viable educational option for students in all 10 Canadian provinces, and in many states in Australia and the USA. Thus, we argue strongly for the need, whenever possible, to set the stage for longitudinal research.

Sustainable Development: An Environmental Perspective

In 1983, the United Nations convened the World Commission on Environment and Development (WCED) to address concerns about the deterioration of environmental and human resources and the consequences of this deterioration on social and economic development. Chaired by Gro Harlem Brundtland, the former Prime Minister of Norway, the commission set out to develop policy for global sustainable development that would ensure environmental protection by the year

2000 and beyond. Now known as the Brundtland Commission, the work of this group resulted in the publication of *Our Common Future* (1987), which raised the public consciousness regarding the concept of sustainability and the factors that must be considered and in place for sustainable development to occur. Although some have argued that the term sustainability has been overused, the United Nations Division for Sustainable Development has listed over 40 areas within the scope of sustainable development. Interestingly, education and awareness fall within the purview of sustainable development policy.

Without entering into too much technical detail, which is beyond the scope of this book, we argue that the theory of sustainable environmental development also applies to developing sustainable intellectual resources in schools. Schools are, after all, ecological environments (Van Lier, 2000) that share many features with interactive environments in the world – they have climate, culture, routine interactive practices, resources and living inhabitants, to name a few. Relating what we know about creating sustainable development in the world might be well worth considering when we examine school-based program sustainability.

The United Nations 2005 World Summit refers to the interdependent and mutually reinforcing pillars of sustainable development as economic development, social development and environmental protection. Figure 8.1 (Adams, 2006) shows the relationship of these three pillars to each other and how the confluence of these pillars leads to sustainability.

Against this backdrop, Agenda 21, a sustainable development program for the 21st century run by the United Nations, insists that for sustainable development to occur, everyone needs to be a user and provider of information on all aspects of the project. In his analysis of this report, Allen (2001) identifies the continual interaction of information, integration and participation as key building blocks to help countries achieve development that renews itself and is permanent. He stresses the need to change from old ways of doing business to new approaches that involve the coordination and the integration of environmental and social concerns into all development processes. Furthermore, Agenda 21 argues for broad public participation in decision making as a fundamental prerequisite for achieving sustainable development. When viewed from the perspective of educational development, we argue that these three pillars and the issues raised in Agenda 21 also apply to creating and predicting sustainable foreign language programs, the topic to which we now turn.

Summary and Conclusions

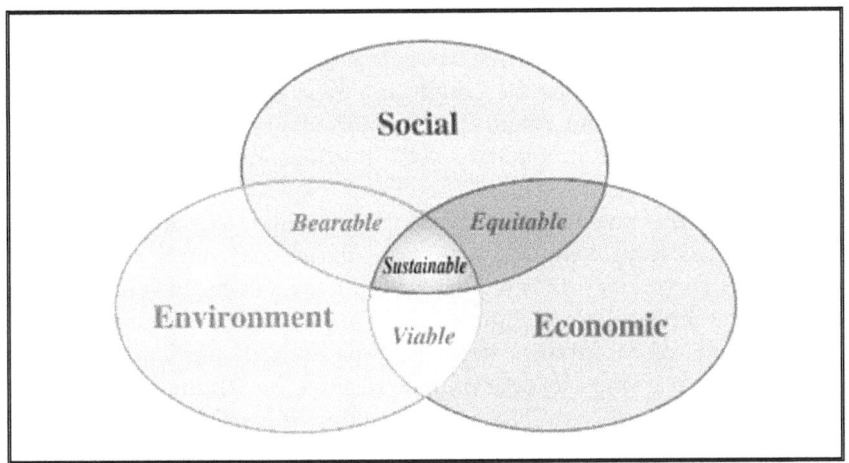

Figure 8.1 The three pillars of sustainable development (Adams, 2006)

As our research has shown, the Spanish program, faced with the pressures of No Child Left Behind (NCLB) and state-mandated testing, remains sustainable and reflects all the features of sustainable development in its planning, implementation and refinement. That is, systematic information was gathered and shared during planning and during program operation, participation was broad-based and decisions were made with input from various constituents, and the program was conceived as an integrated part of the school, as opposed to a novelty, a unique feature or a response to federal funding opportunities.

What is striking is that the Japanese program shares none of the features identified by Allen in his analysis of Agenda 21. Participation in planning was isolated, decision making did not involve the community in which the program was situated and the Japanese program never seemed to find a way to integrate itself into the life of the school. Quite the contrary, as the program moved through the years, its marginality increased and its effectiveness decreased. Japanese classes were reduced to repetitive content across years of instruction often marked by a predominance of the use of English to ensure comprehensibility in mixed classes of cohort and newcomer students.

Referring back to Figure 8.1, we may apply the three pillars to a school system attempting to develop its intellectual resources in global education through the initiation of a sequential K-12 foreign language program for all students. We might make the analogy that school districts, where foreign language study is not systematically offered, are similar to impoverished countries in which people survive on minimal resources for sustenance. As hard as they might try, these districts seem to be at a loss for improving the intellectual conditions of the school district. Beneficial educational innovations seem burdensome, incomprehensible and hard to fathom.

Extending the analogy of a developing country seeking to sustain environmental improvements, a school district may similarly wish to develop its curricular and intellectual resources. Given this analogy, we see how the three pillars in Figure 8.1 are implicated in this process. The development of programs requires broad-based participation and coordination of groups to determine and agree on language of instruction, program model and integration within the existing educational structure. From the perspective of the social dimension, foreign language programs need to be equitable. They must be available to all children who can share in the richness of foreign language instruction. Programs must not demand inordinate economic resources that are taken from other subject areas. That is, in an environment where economic concerns are real, foreign language programs must be economically feasible and must not be seen as a burden on the budget. Rather, the expenses incurred for the program need to be viewed as viable intellectual investments in the school district's academic offerings and in the future of the school district's graduates. In the case of the Spanish program, the expense was often justified by the contribution the program would make to the current curriculum, to the foreign language program as a whole and to the school district's graduates.

Further, federal funding can support the equitable development of programs in all languages, in all schools and for all children. To receive federal assistance, proposal writers should be required to document how newly established elementary school foreign language programs will be sustained as regular curricular offerings. Proposals could require that the architects of new programs address how foreign language study will be anchored in the social, economic and environmental conditions of the school district. Funding sources should also require schools to demonstrate how the needs of all children will be met in foreign language classes, in particular children with learning disabilities. For funding, schools must also demonstrate that they can re-conceptualize the student with a learning disability from a deficient language learner to one that brings a unique and special set of issues to the learning of additional languages.

The social dimension also interacts with the school environment. As Figure 8.1 illustrates, the interaction of the social and the environmental must be bearable in that programs need to respect the existing ecology of the school and need to be respected by this current ecology. If a foreign language program is perceived by other teachers as competing for scant resources or as depleting the time for instruction, sustainability and integration will never be achieved. Thus, foreign language program integration into the environment of the school is critical and must contribute to and support the school's educational mission. This perspective contrasts with language programs that exist on the outskirts of the educational landscape as an isolated enterprise that benefits only a few who are defined as capable of learning a foreign language. Typically, language education programs do not seriously examine their interactions with the school environment. This situation may be why many foreign language programs are the first to disappear when cuts need to be made. Without understanding how foreign language programs interact with the school environment, conflicting and competing educational goals may arise. Although well intentioned, administrators who simply feel the need to board the bandwagon with foreign language instruction, for whatever reason, need to engage in substantive conversations about the environmental effects and resolve the potential conflict of educational, personal and economic goals that a K-12 foreign language program can quite easily engender in the social and physical ecology of the school. We believe the Spanish program was well aware of the interaction of the new program with the existing curriculum in the elementary and middle school. Further, we believe that the program was conceived from the start as an integrated and supportive academic offering of the district's curricular goals. The Spanish program is an illustrative case of how, during planning and implementation, broad-based participation, program integration and information sharing were key features of program development. We conclude that the Spanish program has sustained itself in a way that the Japanese program has not because of the school district's programmatic attention to the interaction of social, environmental and economic factors.

Concluding Remarks

We began this story by framing our research as a tale of two schools. To be fair, although the Japanese program was terminated, the school was well aware of the importance of foreign language study in all grades. Interestingly, the year after the program closed, the director of the school contacted us for advice on how to begin the conversation on building a new K-5 program. We suggested several of the lessons that we had learned from the Spanish program and the director eagerly took our advice. The school sent home a parent questionnaire on choice of language and on parental opinions regarding language study in the elementary grades. A steering committee was established, made up of the middle school Spanish teacher, elementary and middle school subject area teachers, parents and university partners. The head of the middle school chaired the committee, set the agenda for meetings and summarized conversations leading to an action plan. The issue of integration of the language program into the elementary school was discussed and it was decided that the program would link to the major concepts taught across all elementary school subject areas. As the program took shape, information was shared with parents and the rest of the school. When the time came for teacher selection, the search committee included several members of the steering committee. Spanish was selected as the language of study and the program was instituted in 2006 after an intense one-year planning process.

In the summer of 2006, a doctoral student in foreign language education with specialization in early language learning and curriculum development was hired to work closely with the newly hired Spanish teacher to develop a workable K-5 content-based curriculum, with a feasible plan for curricular revision year to year. In the first year of the program, research was conducted on the use of dynamic assessment during whole group instruction, which included the teacher, researchers from Pennsylvania State University and a doctoral student in foreign language education. This research has led to new assessment procedures in the K-5 Spanish program. The research also provided ongoing information on program outcomes in year 1 and a systematic plan for documenting growth in student language proficiency in subsequent years.

It is unclear, at this point, if the new Spanish program in the former Japanese school will sustain itself over time. It appears, however, that, in theory and based on our previous experiences, the program should remain a visible, equal and important part of the elementary school curriculum. Time will tell whether the principles of sustainable program development that we have distilled from our previous work and theory are replicated at this school site. Our tale of two schools concludes, therefore, on a positive note. Although the Japanese school faltered in its initial attempt to implement a program, the lessons learned in the Spanish school contributed to the development of the new program. From all perspectives, we envision that this new K-5 Spanish program will sustain itself in a way that the Japanese program could not. Its development, implementation and monitoring follow closely the planning process in the first Spanish school. Perhaps, in time, our tale of two schools will not be a narrative of stark contrast but one of similar success. Our hope is that, in the near future, our professional narrative will be re-written and the tale of two schools will be, in all cases, 'the best of times'.

Appendix A

Modified ACTFL Rubric for the Presentational Mode of Communication of Intermediate Level Learners

Modified ACTFL Rubric for the Presentational Mode

Rating	Exceeds expectations/3	Meets expectations strong/2	Meets expectations weak/1	Does not meet expectations/0
Language function Language tasks that the student is able to handle in a consistent, comfortable, sustained and spontaneous manner: describe, compare, evaluate, explain	– Describes the pictures using different vocabulary related to natural resources: *En la foto hay un molino de viento; la casa tiene energía solar* – Evaluates the different natural resources by comparing them: *La energía solar es mejor que el petróleo porque...* – Explains the reasons for evaluation: *La energía solar es mejor que el petróleo porque es renovable...* – Uses the connector '*porque*' to make text more cohesive – Expands in quantity and quality	– Describes the pictures using different vocabulary related to natural resources. – Evaluates the different natural resources by comparing them – Falls short of explaining the reasons for evaluation. Does not elaborate using '*porque*' – Few uses of the connector '*porque*' to make text more cohesive – Expands in quantity and quality	– Describes the pictures using different vocabulary of natural resources – Few comparisons used – Does NOT explain the reasons for evaluation. Does not elaborate using '*porque*' – Does NOT use the connector '*porque*' to make text more cohesive – Very few sentences creating meaning in a basic way	– Stays at the description level without using comparing or evaluating – Mostly memorized language with some attempts to create

(Continued)

Rating	Exceeds expectations/3	Meets expectations strong/2	Meets expectations weak/1	Does not meet expectations/0
Text Type Quantity and organization of the language discourse	– Mostly connected sentences using the connector 'porque' and phrases such as 'en la foto' – Varied sentence structure	– Strings of sentences; *some* connected sentence-level discourse using 'porque' and 'en la foto' – Attempts to vary sentence structure	– Simple sentences and some strings of sentences; does NOT use 'porque' – No variety of sentence types	– Simple sentences and memorized phrases (*la energía solar es mejor que el petróleo*); NO use of 'porque' – No variety of sentence types
Impact Depth of presentation and attention to audience	– Accomplishes task, taking into consideration the reporting nature of the assignment and the Spanish-speaking audience: describes, compares, evaluates and explains	– Accomplishes task, taking into consideration the reporting nature of the assignment and the Spanish-speaking audience: describes, compares, evaluates and attempts to explain reasons	– Simple list of sentences without much consideration of audience – Few evaluations and NO explanations	– Focuses on successful task completion by simply listing with NO comparisons, evaluations or explanations

Modified ACTFL Rubric for the Presentational Mode

(Continued)

Rating	Exceeds expectations/3	Meets expectations strong/2	Meets expectations weak/1	Does not meet expectations/0
Vocabulary	– Uses extensive vocabulary related to natural resources (*petróleo, fósil, energía eólica*), comparisons (*mejor, peor, más seguro*), evaluation (*porque*), verbs (*viene de, produce*) – Most words are spelled correctly with proper accent marks	– Vocabulary is sufficient to provide information and limited explanation. Uses extensive vocabulary related to natural resources (*petróleo, fósil, energía eólica*), comparisons (*mejor, peor, más seguro*) and limited evaluations (*porque*). Few or no uses of verbs (*viene de, produce*) – Few errors in spelling and punctuation	– Vocabulary is sufficient to provide information and limited explanation. Uses extensive vocabulary related to natural resources (*petróleo, fósil, energía eólica*), few comparisons (*mejor, peor, más seguro*); NO evaluations (*porque*); NO uses of verbs (*viene de, produce*) – Few errors in spelling and punctuation	– Vocabulary conveys basic information: natural resources (*petróleo, fósil*, etc.) – Many errors in spelling and punctuation
Comprehensibility Who can understand this person's message?	– Generally understood by those unaccustomed to the speaking/writing of language learners	– Generally understood by those unaccustomed to the speaking/writing of language learners	– Generally understood by those accustomed to the speaking/writing of language learners	– Understood with occasional straining by those accustomed to the speaking/writing of language learners

(Continued)

Rating	Exceeds expectations/3	Meets expectations strong/2	Meets expectations weak/1	Does not meet expectations/0
Language control Accuracy, form, degree of fluency	– Most accurate uses of descriptions: *en la foto hay*; comparisons: *'mejor que'*, *'más seguro que'*; negative sentences: *el petróleo no es renovable*; gender/number agreement: *el sol, los recursos naturales*; verb conjugations: *el sol produce energía solar; usamos la energía eólica*	– Most accurate uses of descriptions: *en la foto hay*; comparisons: *'mejor que'*, *'más seguro que'*; negative sentences: *el petróleo no es renovable*; gender/number agreement: *el sol, los recursos naturales*; few errors in verb conjugations: *el sol produce energía solar; usamos la energía eólica*	– Most accurate when producing simple sentences – Few errors in natural resources vocabulary and comparisons – Few errors in negative sentences – Errors in verb conjugations – Overuse of *'ser'* – Overuse of the verb *'ser'*: *'En la foto es un molino'*	– Mostly accurate with memorized language, including phrases – Many errors in natural resources vocabulary and comparisons – Errors in construction of comparisons – Errors in negative sentences – Errors in verb conjugations – Overuse of *'ser'*

References

Adair-Hauck, B. and Donato R. (2009). PACE: A story-based approach to teaching grammar. In J. L. Shrum and E. W. Glisan (eds) *Teachers' Handbook: Contextualized Foreign Language Instruction K-12* (4th ed.) (pp. 90–114). Boston, MA: Heinle and Heinle.

Adams, W.M. (2006) The future of sustainability: Re-thinking environment and development in the twenty-first century. Report of the IUCN Renowned Thinkers Meeting, 29–31 January 2006. Retrieved on: 2010-07-20. See http://cmsdata.iucn.org/downloads/iucn_future_of_sustainability.pdf

Allen, W. (2007) Learning for sustainability: Sustainable development. On WWW at http://learningforsustainability.net/research/thesis/thesis_ch2.html#lin.

American Council on Teaching of Foreign Languages (1998) *ACTFL Performance Guidelines for K-12 Learners*. Yonkers, NY: Author.

American Council on Teaching of Foreign Languages (1999) *ACTFL Proficiency Guidelines – Speaking*. Yonkers, NY: Author.

Antonek, J.L. (1995) Interactive homework: Linking parents to the foreign language learning of their children. Unpublished doctoral dissertation, University of Pittsburgh.

Antonek, J., Tucker, G.R. and Donato, R. (1995) Interactive homework: Creating connections between home and school. *Mosaic* 2 (3), 1, 3–10.

Antonek, J.L., Tucker, G.R. and Donato, R. (1998) Interactive homework: Creating connections between home and school. In A. Mollica (ed.) *Teaching and Learning Languages* (pp. 169–184) (2nd edn). Editions Soleil (reprinted from *Mosaic*). Welland, Ontario.

Asher, J.J. (2000) *Learning Another Language through Actions* (6th ed.). Los Gatos, CA: Sky Oaks.

Baranick, W. and Markham, D. (1986) Attitudes of elementary school principals toward foreign language instruction. *Foreign Language Annals* 19, 481–489.

Bruck, M., Lambert, W.E., Tucker, G.R. and Bowen, J.D. (1975) The 1968 NDEA Philippine Institute for TESL teachers: A follow-up evaluation. *Foreign Language Annals* 8, 133–137.

Cameron, L. (2001) *Teaching Languages to Young Learners*. Cambridge: Cambridge University Press.

Carroll, J.B. (1967) *The Foreign Language Attainments of Language Majors in the Senior Year: A Survey conducted in U.S. Colleges and Universities*. Cambridge, MA: Harvard University Graduate School of Education.

Cekaite, A. (2007) A child's development of interactional competence in a Swedish L2 classroom. *Modern Language Journal* 91 (1), 45–61.

Center for Applied Linguistics (2007) Foreign Language Assessment Directory. On WWW at http://www.cal.org/CALWebDB/FLAD. Accessed 4.2.07.

Cheshire, J. (ed.) (1991) *English Around the World: Sociolinguistic Perspectives*. Cambridge: Cambridge University Press.

Chinen, K., Donato, R., Tucker, G.R. and Igarahsi, K. (2003) Looking across time: Documenting middle school Japanese FLES students' attitudes, literacy and oral proficiency. *Learning Languages* 8 (2), 4–10.

Clark, J.L.D. (1981) Language. In T.S. Barrows (ed.) *College Students' Knowledge and Beliefs: A Survey of Global Understanding* (pp. 25–35, 87–100). New Rochelle, NY: Change Magazine.

Clyne, M., Jenkins, C., Chen, I.Y., Tsokalidou, R. and Wallner, T. (1995) *Developing Second Language Proficiency from Primary School: Models and Outcomes*. Canberra, Australia: National Languages and Literacies Institute of Australia.

Collier, V.P. (1991) A synthesis of studies examining long-term language minority student data on academic achievement. *Bilingual Research Journal* 16 (1&2), 187–212.

Collier, V.P. and Thomas, W.P. (2004) The astounding effectiveness of dual language education for all. *NABE Journal of Research and Practice* 2 (1), 1–20.

Comrie, B. (ed.) (1987) *The World's Major Languages*. New York: Oxford University Press.

Cooper, R.L. (1990) *Language Planning and Social Change*. Cambridge: Cambridge University Press.

Cummins, J. (1979) Cognitive/academic language proficiency, linguistic interdependence, the optimum age question and some other matters. *Working Papers on Bilingualism* 19, 121–129.

Crystal, D. (1987) *The Cambridge Encyclopedia of Language*. Cambridge: Cambridge University Press.

Curtain, H.A. and Dahlberg, C.A. (2004) *Languages and Children—Making the Match* (3rd edn). Boston, MA: Pearson.

Davin, K. (2009) A comparison of the history of early language learning programs in the UK and the US. Unpublished paper, University of Pittsburgh.

Denzin, N. and Lincoln, Y. (eds) (2002) *The Handbook of Qualitative Research* (2nd edn). Thousand Oaks, CA: Sage.

Dickson, P. and Cumming, A. (eds) (1996) *Profiles of Language Education in 25 Countries*. Slough, UK: National Foundation for Educational Research.

Domínguez, R. (2003a) Curricular innovation in elementary school: A case for Spanish literacy. Unpublished doctoral dissertation, Carnegie Mellon University.

Domínguez, R. (2003b) What may lead FL teachers to adopt a new teaching methodology? *Pennsylvania Language Forum* LXXIII (1), 66–78.

Domínguez, R. (2004) From teachers' theory to teachers' practice: How do teachers learn?: A case study of two Spanish teachers in the elementary school. *NECTL Review*, 34–43.

Domínguez, R., Donato, R. and Tucker, G.R. (2005) Documenting curricular reform: Innovative foreign language education for all children. In D. Atkinson, P. Bruthiaux, W. Grabe and V. Ramanathan (eds) *Studies in Applied Linguistics: English for Academic Purposes, Discourse Analysis, and Language Policy and Planning. Essays in Honor of Robert B Kaplan on the Occasion of his 75th Birthday* (pp. 56–71). Clevedon: Multilingual Matters.

References

Donato, R. (1998) Assessing the foreign language abilities of the early language learner. In M. Met (ed.) *Critical Issues in Early Second Language Learning* (pp. 169–197). Glenview, IL: Scott Foresman-Addison Wesley.

Donato, R. (2002) Building knowledge, building leaders: Collaborating for research and change. In L. Wallinger (ed.) *Teaching in Changing Times: The Courage to Lead* (pp. 89–119). Boston, MA: McGraw Hill.

Donato, R. (December, 2003) Action Research. Eric Digest, EDO-FL-03-08.

Donato, R., Antonek, J. and Tucker, G.R. (1994) A multiple perspectives analysis of a Japanese FLES program. *Foreign Language Annals* 27, 365–378.

Donato, R., Antonek, J. and Tucker, G.R. (1996) Monitoring and assessing a Japanese FLES program: Ambiance and achievement. *Language Learning* 46 (3), 497–528.

Donato, R., Gaal, R. and Fall, T. (1993) *Legends and Language Learning: Bringing Africa to the French Classroom*. Pittsburgh, PA: Pittsburgh Public Schools and University of Pittsburgh.

Donato, R. and Terry, R.M. (eds) (1995) *Foreign Language Learning: The Journey of a Lifetime*. Lincolnwood, IL: National Textbook Company.

Donato, R., Tucker, G.R., Wudthayagorn, J. and Igarashi, K. (2000) Converging evidence: Attitudes, achievements and instruction in the later years of FLES. *Foreign Language Annals* 33 (4), 377–393.

Dörnyei, Z. (2001) *Motivational Strategies in the Language Classroom*. Cambridge: Cambridge University Press.

Dörnyei, Z. (2005) *The Psychology of the Language Learner: Individual Differences in Second Language Acquisition*. Mahwah, NJ: Lawrence Erlbaum.

Draper, J. and Hicks, J.H. (2002) Foreign language enrollments in public secondary schools, Fall 2000. On WWW at http://www.actfl.org/i4a/pages/index.cfm?pageid=3389.

Dutcher, N. in collaboration with Tucker, G.R. (1994) *The Use of First and Second Languages in Education: A Review of Educational Experience*. Washington, DC: World Bank, East Asia and the Pacific Region, Country Department III.

Edwards, J. (1994) *Multilingualism*. London and New York: Routledge.

Eggington, W.G. (2005) Language policy and planning: Introduction. In P. Bruthiaux, D. Atkinson, W. Eggington, W. Grabe and V. Ramanathan (eds) *Directions in Applied Linguistics* (pp. 223–226). Clevedon: Multilingual Matters.

Fall, T., Adair Hauck, B. and Glisan, E. (2007) Assessing students' oral proficiency: A case for on-line testing. *Foreign Language Annals* 40 (3), 377–406.

Francis, D.J., Fletcher, J.M., Stuebing, K.K., Davidson, K.C. and Thompson, N.M. (1991) Analysis of change: Modeling individual growth. *Journal of Counseling and Clinical Psychology* 59, 27–37.

Fraser, C., Bellugi, U. and Brown, R. (1963) The control of grammar in imitation, comprehension and production. *Journal of Verbal Learning and Verbal Behavior* 2, 121–135.

Freeman, D. (1998) *Doing Teacher Research: From Inquiry to Understanding*. Boston, MA: Heinle & Heinle.

Freeman, D. (2000) Imported theories/local understandings. *TESOL Matters* 10 (4), 1, 6.

Fullan, M. (2000) *Change Forces, the Sequel*. Philadelphia, PA: Falmer Press, Taylor & Francis.

Furman, N., Goldberg, D. and Lusin, N. (2007) Enrollments in languages other than English in United States institutions of higher education, Fall 2006. The Modern Language Association: web publication, 13 November 2007. http://www.mla.org/pdf/06enrollmentsurvey_final.pdf

Gardner, R.C. (1985) *Social Psychology and Second Language Learning: The Role of Attitudes and Motivation*. London: Edward Arnold.

Gardner, R.C. and Smythe, P.C. (1981) On the development of the Attitude/Motivation Test Battery. *Canadian Modern Language Review* 37, 510–525.

Genesee, F. (1987) *Learning through Two Languages*. Cambridge, MA: Newbury House.

Genesee, F., Lindholm-Leary, K., Saunders, W.M. and Christian, D. (2006) *Educating English Language Learners*. Cambridge: Cambridge University Press.

Glisan, E.W., Adair-Hauck, B., Koda, K., Sandrock, S.P. and Swender, E. (2003) *ACTFL Integrated Performance Assessment*. Yonkers, NY: ACTFL.

Gori, K.H. (2002) Making the link between enrollment and learning goals: A school district's impact. *The Modern Language Journal* 86 (4), 613–615.

Graddol, D. (1997) *The Future of English*. London: British Council.

Graddol, D. (2006) *English Next: Why Global English May Mean the End of 'English as a Foreign Language'*. London: British Council.

Hall, J.K. (1995) "Aw, man, where you going?": Classroom interaction and the development of L2 interactional competence. *Issues in Applied Linguistics* 6 (2), 37–62.

Halliday, M.A.K. (1975) *An Introduction to Functional Grammar* (2nd edn). London: Edward Arnold.

Hamayan, E. (1998) Painting the chameleon: A response to "assessing foreign language abilities of the early language learner" by Richard Donato. In M.C. Met (ed.) *Critical Issues in Early Second Language Learning: Building for our Children's Future* (pp. 176–179). Glenview, IL: Addison-Wesley.

Hardy Dan (April 18, 2008) Loss of mandate riles proponents. *Philadelphia Inquirer*. On WWW at http://www.philly.com/inquierer/education/school_report_card17478619.html.

Heining-Boynton, A.L. and Haitema, T. (2007) A ten-year chronicle of student attitudes toward foreign language in the elementary school. *Modern Language Journal* 91 (2), 149–168.

Hendry, H. (2009) Foreign language learning of students with language learning disabilities: An activity theory perspective of twelve middle school students. Doctoral dissertation, unpublished dissertation University of Pittsburgh.

Holliday, A. (1994) *Appropriate Methodology and Social Context*. New York: Cambridge University Press.

Hudson, J. and Shapiro, L. (1991) From knowing to telling: The development of children's scripts, stories, and personal narratives. In A. McCabe and C. Peterson (eds) *Developing Narrative Structure* (pp. 89–136). Hillsdale, NJ: Lawrence Erlbaum.

Igarashi, K., Wudthayagorn, J., Donato, R. and Tucker, G.R. (2002) What does a novice look like? Describing the grammar and discourse of young learners of Japanese. *Canadian Modern Language Review* 58 (4), 526–554.

Johnson, M. (2001) *The Art of Non-conversation: A Reexamination of the Validity of the Oral Proficiency Interview*. New Haven, CT: Yale University Press.

Johnson, K. and Swain, M. (1997) *Immersion Education: International Perspectives*. New York: Cambridge University Press.
Kennedy, A.M., Mullis, I.V.S., Martin, M.O. and Trong, K.L. (eds) (2007) *PIRLS 2006 Encyclopedia: A Guide to Reading Education in the Forty PIRLS Countries*. Chestnut Hill, MA: International Study Center, School of Education, Boston College.
Kozol, J. (2007) *Letters to a Young Teacher*. New York: Crown.
Lambert, W.E. (ed.) (1984) An overview of issues in immersion education. In *Studies on Immersion Education: A Collection for United States educators*. Sacramento, CA: California State Department of Education.
Lambert, W.E. and Tucker, G.R. (1982) Graduates of early French immersion. In G. Caldwell and E. Waddell (eds) *The English of Quebec: From Majority to Minority Status* (pp. 259–277). Lennoxville, Que.: Institut Quebecois de recherche sur la culture.
Lantolf, J.P. (2003) Intrapersonal communication and internalization in the second language classroom. In A. Kozulin, B. Gindis, V.S. Ageyev and S.M. Miller (eds) *Vygotsky's Educational Theory in Cultural Context* (pp. 349–370). New York: Cambridge University Press.
Lantolf, J. and Poehner, M.E. (2007) *Dynamic Assessment in the Foreign Language Classroom: A Teacher's Guide*. University Park, PA: CALPER.
Lapkin, S. (1998) *French Second Language Education in Canada: Empirical Studies*. Toronto: University of Toronto Press.
Lipton, G. (1998) *Practical Handbook to Elementary Foreign Language Programs (FLES*): Including FLES, FLEX, and Immersion Programs*. Chicago, IL: National Textbook Company.
Markee, N. (1997) *Managing Curricular Innovation*. New York: Cambridge University Press.
Met, M. (1998) *Critical Issues in Early Second Language Learning*. Glenview, IL: Addison-Wesley.
National Standards in Foreign Language Education Project (NSFLEP) (2006) *National Standards for Foreign Language Learning in the 21st Century*. Lawrence, KS: Allen Press.
OECD (2005) *PISA 2003 Technical Report*. Paris: Organisation for Economic Cooperation and Development.
Ogawa, R.T. and Bossert, S.T. (2000) Leadership as an organizational quality. In *The Jossey-Bass Reader on Educational Leadership* (pp. 38–58). San Francisco, CA: Jossey-Bass.
Oliver, R. (1998) Negotiation of meaning in child interactions. *The Modern Language Journal* 82 (3), 372–386.
Oller, J.W. (1998) Assessing early language abilities: A response. In M. Met (ed.) *Critical Issues in Early Second Language Learning: Building for Our Children's Future* (pp. 179–185). Glenview, IL: Scott Foresman.
Omaggio, A. (1993) *Teaching Language in Context*. Boston, MA: Heinle & Heinle.
Padilla, A.M. and Sung H. (1995) The role of student motivation, parental attitudes and involvement in the learning of Asian languages in the elementary and secondary schools. Unpublished research report, Stanford University.
Peabody Picture Vocabulary Test (2006) White Plains, NY: Pearson Assessment.
Pessoa, S., Hendry, H., Donato, G.R., Tucker, G.R. and Lee, H. (2007) Content based instruction in the foreign language classroom: A discourse perspective. *Foreign Language Annals* 40 (1), 102–121.

Pufahl, I., Rhodes, N.C. and Christian, D. (2000) Foreign Language Teaching: What the United States Can Learn from Other Countries. Report prepared for the US Department of Education's Comparative Information on Improving Education Practice Working Group 4. Policy Priority: Foreign Language Learning. Washington, DC: Center for Applied Linguistics. On WWW at http://www.cal.org/ericcll/countries.html.

Reagan, T.G. and Osbourne, T.A. (2002) *The Foreign Language Educator in Society: Toward a Critical Pedagogy*. Mahwah, NJ: Lawrence Erlbaum.

Reitlinger, R. and Foster, A. (2006) Early language learners go to high school: What skills do they bring?. Paper presented at the Annual Pennsylvania State Modern Language Association Conference, Erie, PA.

Rhodes, N.C. and Branaman, L.E. (1999) *Foreign Language Instruction in the United States: A National Survey of Elementary and Secondary Schools*. Washington, DC and McHenry, IL: Center for Applied Linguistics/Delta Systems.

Rosenbusch, M. (1991) Elementary school foreign language: The establishment and maintenance of strong programs. *Foreign Language Annals* 24, 297–314.

Rosenbusch, M. (1995) Language learning in the elementary school: Investing in the future. In R. Donato and R.M. Terry (eds) *Foreign Language Learning: The Journey of a Lifetime* (pp. 1–36). Lincolnwood, IL: National Textbook Company.

Rosenbusch, M. and Jensen, J. (2005) Status of foreign language programs in the NECTFL states. *NECTFL Review* 56, 26–37.

Rosenthal, R. and Jacobson, L. (1992) *Pygmalion in the Classroom* (expanded edn). New York: Irvington.

Rowlands, D. (1972) Toward F.L.E.S. in Great Britain, Part 1. *The Modern Language Journal* 56 (1), 13–20.

San Jose, CA Unified School District. n.d. The Student Oral Language Observation Matrix (SOLOM).

Sapienza, B.A., Donato, R. and Tucker, G.R. (2006) A district-wide foreign language program reaches the middle school: Learning a "second foreign language". *Language Educator* 1 (5), 24–27.

Schiffrin, D. (1987) *Discourse Markers*. Cambridge, MA: Cambridge University Press.

Schweinhart, L.J. and Weikart, D.P. (1997) The High/Scope Preschool Curriculum Comparison Study through age 23. *Early Childhood Research Quarterly* 12, 117–143.

Shohamy, E. (1993) *The Power of Tests: The Impact of Language Tests on Teaching and Learning*. Washington, DC: National Foreign Language Center.

Shrum, J. and Glisan, E. (2009) *Teacher's Handbook: Contextualized Foreign Language Instruction* (4th ed.) Boston, MA: Heinle & Heinle.

Summer Institute of Linguistics (1995) *A Survey of Vernacular Education Programming at the Provincial Level within Papua New Guinea*. Ukarumpa, Papua New Guinea: Summer Institute of Linguistics.

Swender, E. and Duncan, G. (1998) *ACTFL Performance Guidelines for K-12 Learners*. Yonkers, NY: ACTFL.

Terman, L.M. (1925) *Genetic Studies of Genius. Mental and Physical Traits of a Thousand Gifted Children* (Vol. 1). Stanford, CA: Stanford University Press.

Terman, L.M. and Olden, M.H. (1959) *Genetic Studies of Genius. The Gifted Group at Mid-life: Thirty-five Years' Follow-up of the Superior Child* (Vol. 5). Stanford, CA: Stanford University Press.

Tucker, G.R. (1999) The applied linguist, school reform, and technology: Challenges and opportunities for the coming decade. *CALICO Journal* 17 (2), 1–25.

Tucker, G.R. and Donato, R. (2003) Implementing a district-wide foreign language program: A case study of acquisition planning and curricular innovation. In D. Tannen and J.E. Alatis (eds) *Georgetown University Roundtable on Languages and Linguistics 2001, Linguistics, Language, and the Real World: Discourse and Beyond* (pp. 178–193). Washington, DC: Georgetown University Press.

Tucker, G.R., Donato, R. and Antonek, J.L. (1996) Documenting growth in a Japanese FLES program. *Foreign Language Annals* 29 (4), 539–550.

Tucker, G.R., Donato, R. and Murday, K. (2001) The genesis of a district-wide Spanish FLES program: A collaborative achievement. In R.L. Cooper, E. Shohamy and J. Walters (eds) *New Perspectives and Issues in Educational Language Policy: A Festschrift for Bernard Dov Spolsky* (pp. 235–259). Philadelphia, PA: John Benjamins.

Van Lier, L. (2000) From input to affordance: Social-interactive learning from an ecological perspective. In J. Lantolf (ed.) *Sociocultural Theory and Second Language Learning* (pp. 254–259). Oxford: Oxford University Press.

Wells, E.B. (2004) Foreign language enrollments in United States institutions of higher education, Fall 2002. *ADFL Bulletin* 35 (2&3), 7–26.

World Bank (1995) *Priorities and Strategies for Education*. Washington, DC: The International Bank for Reconstruction and Development.

World Commission on Environment and Development (1987). *Our Common Future*. Oxford: Oxford University Press.

World Summit Outcome Document (2005) World Health Organization, 15 September 2005. On WWW at http://www.who.int/hiv/universalaccess 2010/worldsummit.pdf.

Wudthayagorn, J. (2000) Attitude and motivation of elementary school students in a Japanese FLES program. Unpublished doctoral dissertation, University of Pittsburgh.

Index

ACTFL. *See* American Council on Teaching of Foreign Languages (ACTFL)
administration
– Spanish program, 154
American Council on Teaching of Foreign Languages (ACTFL), 1, 5, 9, 23, 48, 61
– modified rubric, 166–170
– National Standards, 28
– student writing, 73
American education
– foreign language programs, 7
– K-8 schools, 7
– Spanish program, 138
Amigos program, 57

backwash effect, 34
Brundtland, G.H., 159
Brundtland Commission, 160

CAL. *See* Center for Applied Linguistics (CAL)
CALPER. *See* Center for Advanced Language Proficiency Education and Research (CALPER)
CASL. *See* Center for Advanced Study of Language (CASL)
CBI. *See* content based instruction (CBI)
CEFR. *See* Common European of Reference for Languages (CEFR)
Center for Advanced Language Proficiency Education and Research (CALPER), 4
Center for Advanced Study of Language (CASL), 4
Center for Applied Linguistics (CAL), 9
– *National Survey of Foreign Language Teaching U.S. Schools*, 14
children
– classroom performance, 89
– communicative ability, 51
– foreign language education, 2
– foreign language problems, 6
– Japanese program, 101, 124
– language development, 44, 98
– oral texts, 91

Common European of Reference for Languages (CEFR), 16
communicative ability
– children, 51
content based instruction (CBI)
– foreign language programs, 51
– Spanish program, 60
– teachers, 42
content-related curriculum
– foreign language programs, 31
creative language, 88
curriculum
– diversification, 151
– foreign language programs, 151
– Japanese program, 143

Department of Education and Skills (DfES), 16
documenting language program development, 96–122
– children views, 96–122
– contribution to school life, 113–117
– foreign language role in school life, 113–117
– foreign language teacher as change agent, 118–129
– parents expectations of children's learning, 96
– parents view, 96–122
– students beliefs about languages, 109–112
– students impression of language study, 103–108
– teachers views, 96–122

early foreign language learning (EFLL)
– credibility, 134
– issues, 99
– research challenges, 35–41
– USA, 35
early language learning, 88
– perspectives, 100
– proficiency, 37
early language learning programs, 71, 123–136
– external conditions creating challenges, 129–133

178

– internal conditions creating challenges, 123–128
– sustainability, 123–136
Early Language Learning Research Team (ELLRT), 24
education
– culture assessment, 33
– multiple languages, 12
– programs, 33
EFLL. *See* early foreign language learning (EFLL)
elementary schools
– foreign language programs, 34, 133, 150
– foreign language study, 10–11
– foreign language teaching, 3
– Japanese program, 37, 105
– Spanish program, 37, 137
ELLRT. *See* Early Language Learning Research Team (ELLRT)
England
– early language learning, 16
– National Languages Strategy, 17
Environmental Protection Agency, 52

FLES. *See* foreign language in elementary schools programs (FLES)
FLEX. *See* foreign language exploratory (FLEX)
FLORES. *See* Foreign Language On Request in Elementary Schools (FLORES)
foreign language
– assignments in public secondary schools, 10
– children problems, 6
– documenting language program development, 113–117, 118–129
– educators, 153
– external factors, 129
– method, 55
– PACE, 55
– role in school life, 113–117
– student competence, 65
– teacher as change agent, 118–129
– teachers issues, 38
– teaching in elementary schools, 3
– university partnership, 153
foreign language education, 155
– children, 2
– evaluation comprehensive model, 34
– National Standards for Foreign Language learning, 147
– planning activities, 2
– programs, 2, 34
foreign language exploratory (FLEX), 62

foreign language in elementary schools programs (FLES), 23
– Japan, 97
– student assessments, 36
Foreign Language On Request in Elementary Schools (FLORES), 30
foreign language programs
– academic content, 146
– academics, 81
– acquisition planning, 156
– American K–8 schools, 7
– CBI, 51
– classroom discourse patterns, 89
– content-related curriculum, 31
– credibility, 136
– curriculum diversification, 151
– day-to-day skills, 155
– elementary schools, 34, 133, 150
– internal classroom factors, 40
– internal factors, 123
– kindergarten, 57, 133
– learning strategies, 43
– middle school, 133
– parents, 54
– reading assessments, 40
– school district-university partnership, 153
– staff turnover, 126
– student achievement, 41
– student assessments, 39, 72
– student motivation, 41
– student performance, 81
– student writing, 72, 83
– teachers, 113, 155
– USA, 15
– vocabulary growth, 85
– vocabulary knowledge, 82
– writing assessments, 40, 72, 93t
– writing comprehension, 52
– writing proficiency, 75, 75t–76t
Foreign Language Teaching in U.S. Schools, 14
French school programs, 21
– Spanish program, 134

GCA. *See* growth curve analysis (GCA)
GDP. *See* gross domestic product (GDP)
German school programs, 134
gross domestic product (GDP)
– Pacific Rim countries, 21
growth curve analysis (GCA), 36, 62–67
– definition, 62
– JFL vocabulary, 66
– oral language, 67
– slope measurement, 65t

Holland
- regional dialect, 13

IEP. *See* individualized education plans (IEPs)
implementation contrastive story, 20–32
- and program development, 20–32
implications
- for additional research, 157–158
- for other districts, 156
individualized education plans (IEPs), 130

Japanese foreign language (JFL) program, 22, 60–72, 105
- children, 101, 124
- cornerstones, 20
- creative language production, 87
- curriculum, 143
- curriculum program, 22
- development (1992-2005), 20–23
- differences from Spanish program, 117
- educational experience, 55
- elementary schools, 37, 105
- in elementary schools, 97
- empowerment, 140
- goals, 146–147
- language choice, 152
- language learning experience, 105, 107
- learning disabilities, 44
- learning factors, 108
- longitudinal assessment, 68
- oral language development, 61, 94
- parents, 96, 98, 100, 103
- parents' questionnaire, 97
- planning, 24
- program reduction, 114
- Spanish program, 43
- Spanish program differences, 117
- speaking abilities, 112
- storytelling, 91
- student(s), 54, 71, 110, 128, 144
- student assessments, 35
- student language achievement documentation, 66–67
- student lessons, 149
- student motivation, 104
- student self-assessment, 109, 111
- teachers, 108, 132
- university partnership, 26
- vocabulary development documentation in year 3, 66–67
Japanese Picture Vocabulary Test (JPVT), 63–64, 66
JFL. *See* Japanese foreign language (JFL) program

JPVT. *See* Japanese Picture Vocabulary Test (JPVT)

kindergarten
- foreign language programs, 57, 133
- Spanish program, 84, 102

language. *See also* American Council on Teaching of Foreign Languages (ACTFL); documenting language program development; early foreign language learning (EFLL); early language learning; foreign language; Japanese foreign language (JFL) program; oral language; student language achievement documentation
- choice, 152
- creative, 88
- Japanese program, 152
- learning aptitude, 64
- multiple, 12
- Sweden majority, 13
- written language development, 59, 86–88
language development
- communication modes, 96
- longitudinal studies, 46
language education
- planning, 156
- policies, 18
language learning experience
- Japanese program, 105, 107
language programs, 71, 123–136
- documenting development, 96–122
- teachers, 133
learning disabilities
- children internal factors, 135
- parents, 135
- students, 131
learning strategies
- foreign language programs, 43
lessons learned, 149–155

middle school
- foreign language programs, 133
- Spanish program, 124, 137
Modern Language Association (MLA), 11
modified American Council on Teaching of Foreign Languages rubric, 166–170
- intermediate level learners, 166–170
- for presentational mode of communication, 166–170
multiple languages
- education, 12

National Defense Education Act (NDEA)
 – summer training institute, 159
National Languages Strategy
 – England, 17
National Network for Early Language Learning (NNELL), 1
National Standards for Foreign Language Learning (NSFLL), 9, 11, 147. *See also* American Council on Teaching of Foreign Languages (ACTFL)
National Survey of Foreign Language Teaching U.S. Schools
 – CAL, 14
NCLB. *See* No Child Left Behind (NCLB)
NDEA. *See* National Defense Education Act (NDEA)
NEC. *See* Northeast Conference on the Teaching of Foreign Languages (NEC)
NNELL. *See* National Network for Early Language Learning (NNELL)
No Child Left Behind (NCLB), 33, 127, 129, 161
Northeast Conference on the Teaching of Foreign Languages (NEC), 142
NSFLL. *See* National Standards for Foreign Language Learning (NSFLL)

official languages, 12
oral language
 – assessment, 62
 – GCA, 62
 – observation matrix, 49
 – student performance, 69, 70t
 – use in classroom, 51
oral language development, 38, 75
 – and attitude, 47
 – JFL, 59, 60–65, 68–71, 94
 – student language achievement documentation, 59, 86–88
 – students, 59
Oral Proficiency Interview, 48
oral texts
 – TNR, 49

PACE. *See* Presentation, Attention, Co-construction and Extension (PACE)
Pacific Rim countries
 – GDP, 21
parents
 – foreign language programs, 54
 – Japanese program, 96, 100, 103
 – learning disabilities, 135
 – Spanish program, 96
Peabody Picture Vocabulary Test, 51

Pennsylvania State Modern Language Association (PSMLA), 32, 118, 126, 142
Presentation, Attention, Co-construction and Extension (PACE)
 – foreign language method, 55
 – phases, 120
 – Spanish literacy, 120
 – Spanish teachers, 56, 121
program development, 20–32
 – beginning, 29–32
 – and implementation contrastive story, 20–32
 – Japanese program 1992-2005, 20–23
 – Spanish program 1995-present, 24–28
program emergent themes, 137–148
program evaluation comprehensive model, 33–58
 – areas, 48–56
 – assessment, 34, 35, 45–47, 48–56
 – EFLL research challenges, 35–41
 – foreign language education programs, 34
 – plan, 35
 – principles, 45–47
 – transitions and connections, 42–44
program positioning within school life
 – successful programs emergent themes, 144–147
program visions
 – successful programs emergent themes, 137–139
PSMLA. *See* Pennsylvania State Modern Language Association (PSMLA)
public secondary schools
 – foreign language assignments, 10
Pygmalion effect, 158

reading
 – assessments, 40
 – foreign language programs, 40
 – Spanish program, 119
 – student comprehension skills, 9

school. *See also* elementary schools; foreign language in elementary schools programs (FLES); middle school
 – districts environmental improvements, 162
 – environment, 163
 – secondary, 10
 – social dimensions, 163
secondary schools
 – foreign language assignments, 10
Seven Functions of Language, 74
SFL. *See* systematic functional linguistics (SFL) theory

Singapore
- educational system, 13
skills-based thematic unit approach
- Spanish program, 42
social dimensions
- school environment, 163
SOF. *See* Student Observation Form (SOF)
Spanish
- alphabet writing, 119
- education, 27
- FLES program, 27
- kindergarten, 84
- language teachers, 118
- language teaching specialists, 29
- literacy, 120
- literacy development over time, 72–85
- PACE, 56, 120, 121
- teachers, 56, 121
Spanish program, 21, 103
- administration, 139, 154
- American education, 138
- assessment program, 72
- buildup approach, 38
- CBI, 60
- classroom interaction, 109
- cultural exposure, 103
- development, 24–28, 116
- elementary school, 137
- elementary schools, 37
- English questionnaire, 112
- evolution, 115
- French school programs, 134
- German school programs, 134
- implementation, 141
- Japanese program, 43
- Japanese program differences, 117
- kindergarten, 57, 102
- literacy development, 94
- middle school, 124, 137
- 1995-present, 24–28
- parents, 96
- reading, 119
- school districts, 125, 130, 145
- skills-based thematic unit approach, 42
- speaking abilities, 113
- student(s), 128
- student assessments, 35
- student language development, 71
- student lessons, 149
- student performance, 92
- student questionnaire, 108
- success, 152
- summer programs, 143
- teachers, 127

- writing ability, 95
speaking abilities
- Japanese program, 112
- Spanish program, 113
staff turnover
- foreign language programs, 126
standards-based language teaching
- teachers, 31
storytelling
- Japanese program, 91
- personal narratives, 89
student(s)
- classroom interaction, 87
- foreign language competence, 65
- Japanese program, 54, 128, 144
- learning disabilities, 131
- oral language development, 59
- oral language performance, 69, 70t
- reading comprehension skills, 9
- second language abilities, 44
- written language development, 59
student achievement
- foreign language programs, 41
- grade 4, 69t
- grade 5, 69t
- multiple perspectives analysis, 45
- writing functions, 82
student assessment
- oral, 50
- principles, 48
- writing assessment, 52
student independent performance, 89–95
student language achievement
  documentation, 59–95
- classroom discourse, 89–95
- classroom instruction, 86–88
- cumulative oral language development
  JFL year 1, 59
- cumulative oral language JFL year 3, 62–65
- JFL vocabulary development
  documentation in year 3, 66–67
- oral language development, 86–88
- relationships between discourse and
  performance, 89–95
- relationships between instruction and
  development, 86–88
- Spanish literacy development over time,
  72–85
- student independent performance, 89–95
- written language development, 86–88
student motivation
- foreign language programs, 41
- Japanese program, 104
Student Observation Form (SOF), 49

Index

Student Oral Proficiency Assessment, 45
student performance, 89–95
 – foreign language programs, 81
student self assessment
 – instrument, 109
 – Japanese program, 109, 111
student writing
 – ACTFL, 73
 – foreign language programs, 83
 – functional analysis, 79t
 – language function criterion, 73
 – sentence type comparison, 84t
successful programs emergent themes, 137–148
 – participating students, 142–143
 – program positioning within school life, 144–147
 – program visions, 137–139
 – teacher support, 140–141
sustainable development, 159–162, 161f
Sweden majority language, 13
systematic functional linguistics (SFL) theory, 53

Tale of Two Schools, 1–19
 – essential questions, 6–8
 – international experiences, 12–19
 – rationale, 1–5
 – US experiences, 9–11
teachers
 – CBI, 42
 – as change agent, 118–129
 – foreign language program, 113
 – foreign language programs, 113, 155
 – issues with foreign language, 38
 – JFL program, 108, 132
 – language programs, 133
 – Spanish, 56, 121
 – Spanish program, 127
 – standards-based language teaching, 31

 – support, 140–141
 – views, 96–122
true narrative representations (TNR)
 – oral texts, 49

United States
 – early language learning, 15
 – EFLL, 35
 – foreign language programs, 15
 – taught languages, 101
university partnership
 – foreign language educators, 153

vocabulary
 – foreign language programs, 82, 85
 – growth, 85
 – knowledge, 82
 – syntactic complexity, 85
Vygotskyan psycholinguistics, 55

World Commission on Environment and Development (WCED), 159
writing
 – ability, 95
 – ACTFL, 73
 – foreign language programs, 83
 – functional analysis, 79t
 – language function criterion, 73
 – proficiency, 75, 75t–76t
 – sentence type comparison, 84t
 – Spanish alphabet, 119
writing assessments
 – foreign language programs, 40, 93t
 – student, 52
written language development
 – student language achievement documentation, 86–88
 – students, 59
written text
 – accurate language, 79

For Product Safety Concerns and Information please contact our EU Authorised Representative:

Easy Access System Europe

Mustamäe tee 50

10621 Tallinn

Estonia

gpsr.requests@easproject.com

www.ingramcontent.com/pod-product-compliance
Ingram Content Group UK Ltd.
Pitfield, Milton Keynes, MK11 3LW, UK
UKHW021941200326

4879IPUK00004B/42